NELL'S WAR

REMEMBERING THE BLITZ

BEN WICKS

Stoddart

For my mother, Nell

Copyright © 1990 by Ben Wicks

First published in 1990 by
Stoddart Publishing Co. Limited
34 Lesmill Road
Toronto, Canada
M3B 2T6

CANADIAN CATALOGUING IN PUBLICATION DATA
Wicks, Ben, 1926-
    Nell's war

ISBN 0-7737-2424-9

1. World War, 1939-1945 — Great Britain.
2. World War, 1939-1945 — Aerial operations,
German.   I. Title.

D759.W52 1990   940.53'41   C90-094567-2

DESIGN: ArtPlus Limited/Brant Cowie

Printed in the U.S.A.

CONTENTS

INTRODUCTION

WHEN FRANCE FELL in the summer of 1940, Europe found itself in the hands of one of the greatest armies the world had ever seen. Those given the task of stopping the advance of the forces of Nazi Germany were small in number and occupied a tiny island.

As the Luftwaffe gouged its path of destruction throughout Britain in 1940 and 1941, it seemed that Hitler might succeed in his intent to bring the nation to its knees. But the British on the home front still worked, raised their children and then made their way to crowded underground shelters at night to escape the enemy bombs. Enduring enormous hardship, this army of young and old, men and women, pulled together to protect their homeland.

This is the tale of that army of ordinary people told in their own words. Many of the stories are horrific, many tell of heroism and some even recount the experience with humour.

More than a thousand readers of British newspapers answered my request for true stories of Britain's blitz. A similar notice in the

German press would, I am sure, have brought a response from another civilian population that suffered the horrors of death from the air. I have included a few personal accounts from German pilots who, as attackers, were just as young and innocent and died just as easily as those on the British side.

My mother, Nell, lived through the blitz. Though she is no longer alive, I have a tape of an interview I once had the opportunity to do with her for CBC Television. To watch her tell her story on that tape is still to witness the extraordinary resilience of the ordinary people. She, like most of the poor, were the obvious targets because their homes nestled in the slum areas beside the docks and vital wartime factories. In a special way, this book is Nell's story. Through her eyes we see the small neighbourhood where she lived and watch her neighbours' daily struggle to survive that dreadful time.

PROLOGUE

*S*TEPPING CAREFULLY *between her two daughters and the other sleepers sprawled on the tube train platform, Nell groped her way to the emergency stairs. A light breeze from the street above cut into the stench from toilet buckets hidden behind canvas screens beside the lift doors.*

As she climbed the stairs Nell thought how lucky they were to be living so close to the Borough tube station, a ready-made air-raid shelter. She wondered how her husband, Alf, was sleeping, alone in their tiny flat nearby.

She stopped and took a deep breath. The sounds of the anti-aircraft guns competed with the thud of falling bombs. She adjusted her steel hat and climbed the last few steps into the darkened London street.

It was almost four o'clock in the morning and she quickened her pace. Ten years she'd had the job and never missed a day. Rain or shine, Mr. Perry and his bank staff entered the bank at nine o'clock and walked across floors that had been scrubbed by her and her mates. It was going to take more than a funny little man with half a comb above his lip to make her late.

She looked up at the searchlights picking and poking their way through the night sky. Occasionally a light would reveal a plane. Other lights quickly moved to hold the plane captive in the centre of a huge cross of light.

Nell fastened the strap on her helmet and hurried on. At any minute there would be a shower of shrapnel from the ack-ack guns, which had missed their target once again. She wondered why the gunners bothered tracking a target if they couldn't hit it. She smiled to herself as she thought of the propaganda about how brave the Londoners were and how "the British people could take it." What else could they do? Certainly there was nowhere else to go. London was home. Even if she had a "country place," how would she get there? As for "braving the bombs" to get to work, well, if truth be known, she loved her job. Meeting her mates in the offices was one of the few pleasures this miserable war still allowed her.

A fire engine screamed across a deserted London bridge. New fires lit the skies ahead of her. She hurried across the bridge and turned a corner. A figure stepped into her path.

"Can't go down there, luv." The bobby adjusted the shoulder strap on his gas mask.

"Wot yer mean, I can't go down there? I gets to me work by going down there."

"Then you'll have to go another way."

"Wot other way?"

He pointed. "Go down there and around."

"I'll be late. Wot's wrong wiv me going down there?"

"Well, if you must know, we 'as an unexploded bomb down there, that's wot."

"There'll be an unexploded bomb waiting in the bank if I don't get there in time to do the floors."

"If you don't get out of 'ere soon, luv, you ain't gonna be doing any floors, since you'll be under 'em."

Nell was late that morning, but by the time Mr. Perry had made his way through the streets strewn with broken glass and opened the front door, the floor of his bank was clean.

As Nell left for home she muttered to her friend Flo, "Whoever's responsible for dropping bloody bombs on people should 'ave one drop on them."

1

THE DARKENING CLOUDS

In 1927 A TALL SKINNY American kid fastened the strap of his leather helmet and climbed aboard a single-engine Ryan monoplane in New York. *The Spirit of St. Louis* slowly climbed into the night sky, and 33 hours and 39 minutes later Charles Lindbergh touched down 3600 miles away in Paris. Lindbergh's flight would help create the financial and technical climate for the continued development of aviation. And continue it did. By the 1930s the first long-range bomber had made its appearance.

Germany had been barred from building war planes by the Treaty of Versailles, but this did not mean that they could not produce any aircraft. They developed high-powered sporting, mail and transport planes that could easily be transformed into war machines. Typical of these was the Heinkel 51, a plane so fast and manoeuvrable that it could outfly any fighter. At an air show in 1936, its potential as part of a new and powerful Luftwaffe was suddenly revealed.

The British government, who had done little in 15 years to improve its country's aviation might, panicked, and immediately ordered an expansion of the Royal Air Force.

A battle was brewing, and Britain had yet to put the water in the kettle.

It was 1937. Nell and her family were living in St. George's Buildings, a five-storey block of flats in the borough of Southwark, in the East End of London. Their flat consisted of three tiny rooms, with a bathroom down the hall they shared with other families. Doll, the elder of Nell's two daughters, had met a young man at a local dance hall. Alf, Nell's husband, was not pleased, feeling that his daughter, at 18, was too young to have a boyfriend, but as Nell told him, "Wot are yer talking about? I was only 18 and you was glad enough to take me out."

War in Europe had become a reality. No longer would the battle lines be just drawings on a map of a foreign country.

In 1936, when the Italians used poison gas against a defenceless Abyssinia, a new Germany was rising. A little man with a funny moustache was winning the support of millions of Germans who, unlike the rest of the world, did not see him as a clown. Adolph Hitler's troops goose-stepped into the Rhineland as Franco began his move against the Spanish Republic. Within days, the planes that Goering had been waiting to test against a human target were in the skies over Spain.

News cameras captured the action. Thousands of horrified moviegoers around the world watched the Junker 87s drop screaming bombs on a defenceless population. Yet the German planes were a great disappointment to Goering. Most of the bombs ended up anywhere but on their targets, and the Heinkel 51 biplane proved an inferior fighter to those supplied to the Republicans by Russia. However, with the arrival of the Dornier 17 and Heinkel 111 bombers, faster than the enemy fighters, the brass in Berlin leapt to the jubilant conclusion that their swift bombers would never need fighters to protect them.

It would prove to be a great mistake.

Sydney Camm, the chief designer at the Hawker Siddeley aircraft company, was deep in thought as he made his way home from his office. His newest design for a biplane and monoplane had been rejected by the British Air Ministry. Yet Hawker, aware that in Camm they had a brilliant designer, encouraged him to ignore specifications from the ministry. His mind was spinning with its new-found freedom.

By the time the Air Ministry had revised new specifications Camm had finished the design for a new fighter aircraft. The only difference between what the ministry wanted and what Camm already had on paper was the number of machine guns. In the summer of 1936 his new monoplane was wheeled into view. The Hurricane was born.

Reginald Mitchell, the chief designer at the Supermarine Company on the south coast of England, had designed the sea plane that won the Schneider Cup race in 1931. That same year, his plane, the S6B, had reached speeds of more than 400 miles an hour. Now he was being asked by the Air Ministry to create an equally fast fighter aircraft. In 1932 the ministry agreed to his making a prototype, based on his designs and reports.

A year later, on the continent to convalesce after an operation, Mitchell talked with young German aviators and became convinced that war was on the way. Mitchell threw aside all thought of rest and flung himself into the task of building a plane that would outstrip all others. All that remained was to build and test the Rolls-Royce engine, which everyone agreed was the answer.

The first new engine went straight from the factory into the waiting aircraft.

On March 5, 1936, a car pulled alongside a hangar at Eastleigh airfield in Hampshire. Mitchell, the passenger, shielded his eyes against the sun and watched the Spitfire take to the air for the first time. The designer never knew how grateful his nation would be. Reginald Mitchell died in 1937 at the age of 42.

Nell's husband was employed as a printer and Nell had found work cleaning offices. They'd just moved from their flat with shared toilet at the back of the building into three rooms at the front with its own toilet. Their new neighbours were the Wallaces, a family of 12 living in two rooms separated by a curtain. Mr. Wallace was a hard-working docker who came home most nights via the pub, singing at the top of his voice.

St. George's Buildings, their block of bug-infested flats, were full of poor but friendly neighbours. The paper-thin walls allowed everyone to share everyone else's business. Who had lost or found a job, who was sick and who was healthy, who ate what for supper. Upstairs, Johnnie Basted could be heard every morning shouting to his mother, "Cuppa tea, Muvver!" followed by "Coming, John boy!"

The overcrowding was particularly tough on the women, who had to share the cleaning of the common hallways, stairs and toilets. "Wot d'yer mean, it's my turn to clean the stairs?...I cleaned 'em last week...'Cause it's your turn t' clean the toilet...Wot d'yer mean, I left a stain in the copper?...I cleans the copper when I've finished me wash every time and you knows it...."

Living in such close quarters demanded trust. No door was without its piece of string attached to the lock inside and hanging outside so that with a slight tug even a complete stranger could enter. On Mondays the rent man was always paid five shillings for each flat. Even the local money lender could be sure of being repaid — at least the interest — once a week.

The conditions created a neighbour-support system. When one woman delivered twins, bringing the number in her family to 12, it was the neighbours who pooled what little money they had to supply desperately needed diapers.

Occasionally Nell's husband, Alf, suffering chronic stomach pains from a gas attack in France during the First World War, would call on Dr. Stone around the corner. But there was little the doctor could do, and Alf would fall back on the white stomach powders that coated his stomach yet brought little relief. Night after night Nell's son and daughters would lie awake as their mother worked to make their father more comfortable.

Sometimes the family went on outings to Southend, an hour's train ride from London. One glorious Sunday in June, while Nell prepared a Sunday meal, Alf went off with the children to the mouth of the Thames and headed for the stone-covered beach. The tide was out, but undeterred, they began the mile-long trek to the water. At the water's edge, Alf looked around. Confident that no one could see him, he removed his tie and collar stud, then his shoes and socks. With his trousers rolled up to his knees, he strolled into the shallow lapping water. Snapping his braces, he lifted his chin and loudly declared, "This is the life!"

And so it seemed for many of the working poor.

Others, however, were less content. War appeared inevitable to them, and they could envisage vast numbers of enemy aircraft dropping their bombs indiscriminately on the tiny island.

The government made local authorities responsible for the safety of their residents and set up an organization called Air Raid Precautions — ARP. Its members were air-raid wardens, and despite the fact that few in Britain took their warnings seriously, by the middle of 1937 ARP had recruited about 200,000 civilians.

Doll's new boy-friend joined the Territorial Army. Whether it was the uniform or true love, Doll married him in 1938. He was from the neighbouring borough of Lambeth, the tattered boyhood home of Charlie Chaplin.

In Southwark meanwhile, Ruth Reid, the local money lender, could be found wearing her big apron with its deep pockets and sitting at the end of the long table in the Lord Clyde pub. She was waiting for her customers to pay the interest on their loans. Before they paid, Ruth would always insist they buy her a drink.

The local market was closed on Mondays, and after a weekend of drinking, most of the costermongers were broke by Tuesday when they desperately needed funds to buy new produce. At four o'clock in the morning along would come Ruth, ready to lend a hand with her high-interest loans.

In response to the growing crisis in Europe, the British government started to re-arm. A quarter of the nation's budget was allocated to defence. An Air Ministry plan to build 12,000 airplanes in three years was put into action after news arrived from the continent that Hitler was the undisputed leader of Germany and determined to establish his people as the "super" race.

In March 1938 Austria fell. In England appeals were made for volunteers to assist with the massive problems the population would face in a war, which seemed almost certain to come.

Lady Reading chaired the newly formed Women's Volunteer Service (WVS) and appealed to women throughout Britain to join.

The air-raid wardens undertook a house-to-house drive for volunteers. The most common response was "What's ARP?" The results of the recruiting drive were not good.

Hitler's invasion of Czechoslovakia spurred the distribution of 38,000 gas masks throughout Britain by thousands of volunteers. Even the prisoners in a Dorchester jail lent a hand.

The threat of war increased the strain of living in the bug-infested rooms of St. George's Buildings. Young Mrs. Collins, on the left-hand ground floor, found she had little in common with the newly arrived Pepperell family, and soon the sounds of screaming echoed up and down the stairways as Mrs. Collins pulled Sally Pepperell's hair. Most arguments began with the children, and this one was no different. Sally Pepperell left the buildings soon after, and weeks later news filtered back that two of her three children, Bobby and Eileen, had died of diphtheria within days of each other.

When, despite the invasion of Czechoslovakia, a jubilant Neville Chamberlain declared, "It is peace for our time," there was a great collective sigh of relief. Even if Britain wanted to take on Germany it was hardly ready to do so.

When Nell and her family unpacked the small cardboard boxes, took out the gas masks and tried them on, they found them very uncomfortable, and the rubber, which clung to the face, gave off a strong odor. At least it wasn't difficult to breathe, and the children had fun making rude noises by forcing air out from the side of the mask, much to their father's disgust. Alf was quite happy to sit quietly reading his newspaper and not concern himself with what only might come.

Nell tried just once to get a gas mask over her hair bun. It wouldn't fit, and she threw the mask to one side in disgust. It seemed most of the neighbours shared Nell's lack of interest in the new-fangled rubber masks. Mr. Tingle, the bookmaker's lookout, needed a clear view of the alley. "Fat chance I've got of spotting the coppers if I got somfink like that on me face."

Although many city dwellers spent their Saturdays filling sand-bags, life in Southwark went on with little change. Mr. Parker, the bookmaker, continued to make use of Mrs. Gaffney's flat on the ground floor of St. George's Buildings.

Mr. Tingle's warning cry of "Heads up!" when a policeman showed his face in the alley would result in the bookie's slamming the door of Mrs. Mead's flat, usually in the poor lookout's face. It was said that Mr. Tingle had lost a leg in the First World War. He certainly had a distinct limp and he rarely made it safely to the bookmaker's flat. Most of the money paid him each week was spent in fines.

13

Alf would pass the Saturday afternoon studying the horses and filling small pieces of paper with dozens of names. He would place a sixpence in the paper and twist it. Nell would lean over the banister, shout to the bookie below and drop the bet into his hands. Alf's bet would be on.

Posters appealing for civil-service volunteers began to appear. One, asking for volunteer firemen to join the Auxiliary Fire Service (AFS), made regular firemen uneasy. They felt threatened by the idea of large numbers learning their trade.

For the men living in St. George's Buildings the AFS held great appeal. One of the largest fire stations in London was located in the area, and even Nell's neighbour, an ex-docker and father of four who was serving six months for stealing a quarter pound of tea, claimed he would volunteer just as soon as he got out of prison.

Women were not neglected in the call for volunteers — telephonists, canteen staff and ambulance drivers were needed. Unfortunately, the poorer areas of Britain were hardly the place to look. Most, like Nell, had never sat in a car, let alone driven one.

Schoolchildren chanted:

> Under the spreading chestnut tree,
> Neville Chamberlain said to me:
> "If you want your gas mask free,
> Join the blinking ARP."

Thousands did join ARP and the organization's budget tripled. More than a quarter of the nation's taxes were thrown into the defence kitty, and with these extra funds a much-needed source of employment was opened up in depressed areas: the production of shipping and munitions. At last the numbers of British aircraft coming off the assembly lines exceeded those of the Germans.

Nell's daughter Doll and Doll's husband, Howard, were woken by a knock on their door at 2 A.M. It was the police, who were there to tell Howard he was needed. He went off to an army camp close to London.

Nineteen thirty-nine was the last year Nell and her family, and many other Cockney families, would have a hop-picking holiday. This annual working holiday brought in extra money and got the kids out into the fresh country air. With her son and two daughters, Nell joined the other women and children in the back of the lorry. As their happy band set off they waved to husbands and fathers staying at home to work. Soon the soot-covered alleyways gave way to the green fields of Kent. It was a glorious summer; and as the part-time farmers from London sat around their camp fires singing songs of the First World War, a second war seemed impossible.

By August recall notices were sent out by the thousands, and men began to make their way to enlistment offices, swelling the ranks of the Territorial Army.

Alice Mulvey was camping in Devon with her sister, her husband, Dick, and a friend:

ONE EVENING it began raining and we decided to take a bed and breakfast, instead of putting up the tents. While we were there that evening we heard that all the reservists were being called up because of the grave situation that faced the country. "That means me," said Dick, whose reserve with the Grenadier Guards was up on September 21. Next morning we went to Hereford to see my parents before heading back to London. That was the last time our whole family (six of us) were together.

Many of the schools began evacuation rehearsals months before the outbreak of war. These usually consisted of assembling the children in the playground and marching them off to the nearest railway station and back.

15

Gordon Tothill, now living in Canada, was attending a school that found a simple solution:

WE DID IT without leaving the school. A teacher stood in one corner of the playground and pointed to the floor and said, "This is the railway station over here." We were then assembled in groups and made to march around the playground to the spot he'd pointed out, stop, turn around and go back to where we'd started, and that was it.

For most people in Britain the war really began not with Chamberlain's announcement but with the sounds of thousands of tiny feet making their way to railway stations throughout the country.

Sending her children away was the last thing Nell wanted. Her only son, who was constantly sick, had developed a bad cough. Stone did his best to persuade Nell that the lad should be in hospital, but she insisted she be allowed to care for him at home. Day and night for two weeks, she slept beside him in front of a fire in the hopes that the cough would disappear. It did not, and finally she was forced to give in to the doctor's wishes. She hurried along beside the stretcher, holding the hand of her son as the sound of the ambulance bell clanged its exit from the alley. The illness, which had left a cloud in his lung, left her no alternative but to send him to Stowey House, an open-air school on the edge of Clapham Common in South London. He would join dozens of others in the area whose lungs were in desperate need of clean air.

The day was not a happy one for the Polish ambassador to Germany. Hitler had given his troops orders to attack Poland, and by early morning they had crossed the frontier. The invasion of Poland had begun.

The sound of bells from nearby St. George's Church drifted down the alley and into Nell's tiny flat. The buildings that usually echoed with the sounds of children playing were strangely quiet now, but for the bells.

With the radio playing in the background, Nell was busy preparing the most important meal of the week, Sunday dinner, and wondering how her son was being treated at his new home in the country. Alf sat quietly by the window trying to read the Sunday papers.

The recorded music was suddenly interrupted by an announcer introducing the prime minister. The 70-year-old leader told the nation that he was speaking from the cabinet room at No. 10 Downing Street and that a state of war now existed between Germany and Britain. After a "God Bless you all" the national anthem was played.

The announcement had been expected, and after a short discussion, Nell and Alf got back to what they had been doing. But shortly afterward, an air-raid siren sounded. Nell and her two daughters made their way downstairs with the rest of the neighbours and stood in the street trying to figure out the location of the nearest air-raid shelter. Alf stayed where he was, reading the paper. After years in the trenches, he needed more than a siren to get him to take cover.

London began to look like a city at war. Posters appealed for volunteers to fill sandbags. Tin hats and gas masks were everywhere, and hundreds of civilians wearing various arm bands patrolled the streets ready to give orders at the first sign of danger.

Thousands of taxi-cabs had been transformed into miniature fire engines, pulling emergency trailers with hoses, axes and rope ladders. Many cars sported stickers to show they belonged to some vital service. Overhead in the clear bright sky floated a flock of large, silver-grey barrage balloons. They were hitched to long, thick cables, waiting to trap the first German aircraft that dared fly too low.

Nell's younger daughter, Nan, had a boy-friend named John, and he threw a kitbag over his shoulder and left for the nearest railway station.

Although he would soon be back on leave it was a tearful parting. Within days of the start of the war, the tiny flat in St. George's Buildings was quieter than it had been in a long, long time.

All places of entertainment were closed, and people were warned to keep off the streets as much as possible, even though there was little that seemed threatening outdoors.

With the blackout in force the whole of Britain found itself living in a dark world punctuated by the cries of local air-raid wardens: "Put that bloody light out!" Black curtains had been made that could easily be pulled across every window. Anyone entering a pub after sunset had to pull aside floor-to-ceiling draperies after opening the door.

The government tried to ease the strain of the blackout. In November 1939 the blackout hours were cut by one hour — a half hour after sunset until a half hour before sunrise.

Although the blackout protected civilians against possible death from the sky, it increased the chances of meeting one's Maker on the ground. With no lights from streets or shops, and few from cars, road accidents quickly doubled.

The government also decided to allow cinemas and theatres to reopen. Football and other spectator sports had ceased for a short period, then were resumed — though stadiums were rarely more than half-filled because, with most of the top players in the armed services, few were willing to pay to see inferior play.

Band musicians and singers suffered, too, as seats in bands were left empty by musicians who had rushed to join the services. One particularly popular singer was Vera Lynn. The public loved her. "We'll Meet Again" had the message that everyone wanted to deliver to a loved one: "Don't be too down, we'll soon be together."

And why not? The whole thing would be over by Christmas, wouldn't it?

At the end of September 1939 ration books were issued. Bacon, sugar and butter were in short supply, and people were told to register with their regular retailer before November 23. The cost of food began to rise, and other irritations such as gasoline rationing quickly followed.

These hardships were difficult to accept, especially by the elderly and unemployed. Why were civilians being asked to make sacrifices when nothing was happening? The air raids had not materialized, and the news from France indicated that the almost 400,000 British soldiers stationed there had little to do but stare at the enemy across a fortified wall.

With the old and unemployed suffering because of increased cost of living, the public increasingly questioned why the government decided to go to war at all.

Morale remained low, and several thousand troops were deployed in London to help the police should the need arise. Top-secret requests were sent to the army: back-up troops would be needed in the event of an emergency.

2

THE

GREAT

ESCAPE

AT **7:30 A.M.** on May 15, 1940, Britain's new prime minister, Winston Churchill, was in a deep sleep at Admiralty House, London, when he awoke with a start. Someone was telling him that the French prime minister was on the phone. He tried to collect his thoughts and concentrate on the voice at the other end struggling to speak English.

"We are beaten," Paul Reynaud blurted into the phone. "We have lost the battle."

"Surely it couldn't have happened so soon?" answered an astonished Churchill.

"The front is broken near Sedan; they are pouring through in great numbers with tanks and armoured cars."

Churchill flew to Paris immediately to see for himself and saw "utter dejection on every face." The British soldiers were in full retreat. German troops were everywhere.

A wire arrived at General Gort's headquarters in France from British Defence Minister Anthony Eden: "Want to make it quite clear that sole task now is to evacuate to England maximum of your force possible."

Gort, commander-in-chief of the British Expeditionary Force (BEF), immediately argued with the French that they should allow their First Army to follow the BEF and make for the French northern seaport of Dunkirk. After much wrangling, General Prioux, commander of cavalry corps, French First Army, ordered General de la Laurencie's 111 Corps to head for the coast. He himself would stay with the rest of his army and fight.

On May 28 Gort set up headquarters in a beach-side villa at the western end of Dunkirk. From there he would direct the greatest escape of all time.

By June 4, with Hitler's army just 10 miles away, 338,000 British troops had scrambled aboard ships of all sizes and made their way back to the safety of Britain's shores. Winston Churchill aptly called the rescue "a miracle of deliverance."

The exhausted, tattered troops from Dunkirk were soon seen all over Britain. Alice Cleary was 10 years old and living in the English seaside town of Ramsgate:

WE LIVED in a large rented house where Mum took in vacationers for bed and breakfast. In early 1940, the many rooms in our house were filled with soldiers training and waiting to be shipped out to an unnamed destination. We had quite a lot of snow that winter and my friends and I would watch the soldiers parading down by the harbour. We would tease them sometimes, and when the parade was over some of them would catch us and playfully rub snow into our faces.

One day in May, our soldier friends went off as usual in the morning and didn't return to our house again. Soon after, my parents and I went down and waited behind the barricade near the harbour to see the men come back from Dunkirk, hoping to see a familiar face in the buses as they went by. Some were wrapped in blankets and bandages, and most were holding cups of hot drinks as they went to the hospital or home.

Sidney Chapman was 17 and had been evacuated to Weymouth, on England's south coast:

WEYMOUTH became a reception area for the French troops and civilians who had escaped across the Channel in a variety of small boats. A number of us were recruited to make use of our limited grammar-school French and help receive these people and compile lists of their names and origins.

Some evacuees like Elsie Kingsland found themselves on trains leaving London as the soldiers were arriving:

WE STOPPED at one station, and on the other side of the platform was another train, and to this day I can remember the soldiers, some bandaged, waving to us — they were on their way home from Dunkirk. We kids were loaded with goodies our parents had given us — chocolate and biscuits — and we threw them onto the platform and the soldiers gratefully picked them up.

George Betts lived in Dover, and his younger brother, Colin, was in the habit of going down to the base of the cliffs at low tide looking for drill bits from a local mining company. Just after Dunkirk Colin told him of a dreadful discovery:

MY BROTHER came running back home to tell us that there was a body on the rocks. The police were at once informed and I went along to investigate.

To our surprise the dead man was over six foot and totally naked apart from his jacket, which was wrapped around his head, held there by the neck button. But the rest of this unfortunate man's body had been badly mutilated by crabs or some other means.

After unwrapping the jacket, which turned out to be from the Royal Marines, we found that the head and facial features were perfectly preserved. It was finally deduced that the man was one of the Dunkirk unfortunates.

Nan Wilson (now Lee) was just six years old when war was declared. Her father had gone to France and her mother was one of the thousands anxiously waiting for news of their loved ones as the retreat from Dunkirk was taking place:

DADDY CAME HOME. He had been one of the lucky ones picked up by a small boat. He had arrived home still in his very soiled, muddy uniform. We were all so happy to see him. He had only been home a few hours when there was a knock at the door.

His best pal had come to give Mum the news that Dad had not been able to make it — he had last seen Dad on the beach. Well, I shall never forget the way those two grown men fell into each other's arms. It is very hard to describe. Dad's pal brought with him a doll dressed in the traditional French costume. I remember it well. It was from Nantes. My name is Nan, and Dad had given it to his pal to bring home to me.

One of the many pubs in Nell's area was close to Waterloo tube station, from where many troops had left for France. Now they were coming back into the same station, a tired and beaten army. As they crowded the bar, the "governor" of the pub climbed onto the counter and declared that drinks were on the house for the rest of the night. The troops may have been beaten, but they had returned to a hero's welcome.

The rescue of the BEF at Dunkirk had resulted in dozens of ships making their way to Dover, and the port became perhaps the busiest in the British Isles.

With the fall of France, Dover had also become the closest point to enemy territory. Luftwaffe aircraft filled the skies above the town, and England's newest "front line" was nicknamed "Hell Fire Corner."

As a worker in the Eastern Docks at Dover, George Betts remembers the arrival of the boats from Dunkirk and the Battle of Britain that followed:

SMALL AND LARGE BOATS emptied their cargoes of British, French, Belgian and other Allied troops, and it was easily seen just what they had been through.

Once, when a motor torpedo boat started up its engines to roar across the harbour to get out of the eastern entrance (the western entrance was blockaded) a great number of these unfortunate men, thinking the engine noise was German planes bombing them, threw themselves to the ground in panic.

This was a good indication of what these troops had been through whilst waiting on the beaches of Dunkirk for the boats to return them to England.

I saw one destroyer towed into the Eastern Docks with its stern blown completely off and another one docked with its bridge almost blown away and shell fragments mingled with blood, plainly showing that this gallant ship had been in battle. Everyone realized that it was now England's turn to be invaded. The Nazi hordes were now only 25 miles from Dover.

Barrage balloons were put up around Dover and its docks to ward off the dreaded dive bombers, but it soon became painfully clear that we hadn't much in those days to stop anything.

Several anti-aircraft guns were manned on the promenade, but these were very few as most of them had been taken to help London.

One morning, just after Dunkirk, I climbed up into a cave where I knew a machine gun had been installed. I was confronted

by several worried gunners who said they hadn't much ammunition and that the gun was firing on a fixed line just to the
bend of the eastern arm pier.

As soon as the Nazis had established airfields in France they
began. First the yellow-nosed Messerschmitts would zoom over,
knocking down all the balloons, as well as machine-gunning the
town and harbours and anyone seen moving.

Then would come the dreaded Stukas, mainly hitting the
harbour, but now and again demolishing houses. The air-raid
shelters around Dover were particularly good, with some being
built into the cliffs directly under Dover Castle.

*Nell managed to scrape up sufficient money to visit her son. He'd
since been moved from Clapham Common to Eastbourne. He spent
the day showing her around the coastal town, but he limped most of
the time because the heels of his feet stuck out of shoes that were
much too small. The worry of how to get new shoes to him put most
of the bad news from France on a back burner for Nell.*

Despite the glorious summer London was dull and drab from the
sacrifices being made to turn around a battle that was not going
well. Even the parks had their decorative railings ripped away,
because the metal was needed for war materials to defeat an
enemy that had made incredible gains.

Although suffering a disastrous campaign in Norway, Churchill
had successfully covered his tracks from the view of the general
public and in May had been able to form a coalition government
under his leadership.

The lightning thrust of Hitler's armies across France had forced
the British to desert their closest ally and make their way back to
the limited safety of their home base. To Churchill's credit he did
not attempt to cloak the defeat of Dunkirk in any other terms than
a major setback. Few doubted that the coming months and maybe
years would be a time when they would find themselves in the
front line of the battle to defend Britain.

3

A TIME TO GET READY

CHURCHILL, LOCKED AWAY in his private thoughts of winning a war against Hitler, noticed little of the drab life of the capital city in the weeks following the withdrawal from Dunkirk. The shops were empty and the roads deserted, but Churchill rarely, if ever, visited a store and certainly had never ridden on a bus. The changes that were causing hardships to families throughout the country were not being experienced by the occupants of No. 10 Downing Street.

Those whose daily lives now consisted of tearing tiny stamps from books to buy food and clothing were doing so in order to preserve a way of life that had long been enjoyed only by a chosen few. As the first Lord Birkenhead once remarked, "Mr. Churchill's tastes are simple. He is easily contented with the best of everything."

For the anticipated coming bombing the prime minister had taken steps to protect himself, his officials and his friends. Deep bunkers were built and amply stocked with provisions.

By the first week in July, work on the Central War Room had been completed, and a satisfied prime minister steered Lord Beaverbrook and General Ironside, the army commander-in-chief, across the courtyard of the Foreign Office and down for an inspection of the underground bunker. The rooms above had been emptied and 16 feet of concrete added for extra bomb-proofing.

Lord and Lady Halifax, Duff Cooper, Somerset Maugham and others of the wealthier classes whose work in London prevented them from escaping to their country manors could always go to the sturdy Dorchester Hotel, with its shatter-proof windows, for an entertaining evening with the finest of food.

The Whites' lodging house on Marshalsea Road was as full as ever. The unemployed had numbered over a million at the outbreak of war, and although jobs were now a little easier to find, many continued to prefer the life of the open road.

It was still only two pence to sleep standing up in the basement. Clotheslines had been strung at shoulder height across the room. By looping your arms over two of them sleep was possible. It was warm and dry, but mostly it was cheap, and there were few nights when there was room "on the line." Those fortunate enough to have sixpence preferred a bed upstairs. The greatest sin in the lodging house was bed-wetting. Anyone who did was immediately thrown out and told never to return. The cleaning man had a nasty little trick. He would urinate in a small urn in the night and pour a little on the sheets of a sleeping man. Early next morning he would wake the poor fellow with the terrible lie that he'd wet the bed. For a few coppers he would keep the dreadful news to himself.

Meanwhile, Nell was busy consoling Mrs. Thurbin, who lived along the landing. Two of the woman's sons had decided to join the services and were about to leave. Nell knew how it felt to have a son leave and although hers seemed safe in the countryside, she missed him dreadfully.

Many Londoners began to look to the skies for the first sign of enemy bombers. They'd gas-proofed their rooms with cellulose sheets and tape; if a family was fortunate enough to have a garden, an Anderson shelter, supplied free by the government, was erected.

The Anderson shelter was not easy to put together. First, a hole measuring seven and a half by six feet had to be dug to a depth of four feet. Then, six curved steel sheets, bolted together to form an arch, were placed over the hole. At either end was a flat steel plate, which could be unbolted to allow entry and exit. It was designed to shelter six people, but when the bombs fell, many were crammed with twice that number.

In March 1941 another type of shelter, the Morrison, was introduced. It consisted simply of a large slab of steel that stood on four sturdy legs and was reinforced with wire mesh, which a family could set up in the house and shelter beneath during a raid. During the all-clear, it could double as a kitchen table.

Mae Wilson was one of eight children. Her father, a scrap-metal merchant in Bootle, near Liverpool, quickly set about protecting his home:

DAD HAD BEEN in the First World War and had lost his leg over in France. He was considered to be a very fine air-raid warden, and despite his wooden leg could climb steps and ladders quicker than anyone else.

When the first air-raid warning was sounded we were in the act of putting brown sticky paper on the windows. As a young girl it was only play-acting to me and I didn't know why I had to put it on the windows, anyway, in that peculiar pattern, and could have thought of much more fanciful patterns to use. Mum ticked me off and said it had to go criss-crossed so that the glass wouldn't splinter and fly all over the room when bombs were coming down. We all got glass splinters as time went on.

For those living in the East End of London, church was not a popular pastime. Most found it a convenient place to send the children on a Sunday afternoon so that the men could sleep off the results of a Sunday lunch spent in the local pub. Certainly Nell knew where to find Alf on any given Sunday. A glance out of the window up the alley at two o'clock would reveal Alf coming home with a glow. This was the signal to start getting the main meal of the week on the table.

Despite the news from France, a peculiar sense of strength pervaded the British with the appointment of Winston Churchill as prime minister. Ernest Bevan, a trade-union leader and champion of the poor, along with other labour members, made up the bulk of the new Cabinet. The poor felt at long last that they were being represented by someone who understood their problems.

But it was Churchill with his magnificent speeches that had Alf glued to the radio set and Nell hushing the two daughters. "I have nothing to offer but blood, toil, tears and sweat," he boomed. Even Alf, a life-long socialist, was moved to nod his head in agreement. The moment the speech was over Alf wrote a letter to his son, who was living with new parents on the south coast, closer to the enemy than anyone in the country.

It was a great relief to learn that the child evacuees were being transferred to other parts of the country, and both Nell and Alf spent anxious days waiting to hear about their 12-year-old's next "posting."

The news that France had signed an armistice with Germany cast gloom over Britain. To counter this, Churchill gave one of his greatest speeches, which transformed a nation of disappointed souls to ones filled with determination:

LET US BRACE ourselves to our duties, and so bear ourselves that, if the British Empire and its Commonwealth last for a thousand years, men will say, "This was their finest hour."

In the dock area of the East End, the feeling was one of gloom mixed with a certain relief and new purpose. "Now we know where we are! No more bloody Allies!" a tugboat skipper called out across the Thames.

Johnnie Basted, the teenage member of the family of 12 in the flat next door to Nell's, had pushed his Bing Crosby records to one side in favour of Vera Lynn's. Nell could hear her voice hour after hour making its way through the thin walls: "There'll be bluebirds over/ the white cliffs of Dover/tomorrow, just you wait and see."

Nell's only interest in birds was Joey, the canary she kept in a cage that hung from a nail driven into the sooty brickwork outside the window. Joey had been a present for their evacuee son, bought on a Sunday morning in Petticoat Lane market.

Though it was said that in this particular market sparrows were caught at one end of Petticoat Lane, sprayed with golden paint and sold as canaries at the other end, Joey was the genuine article and a good match for Vera Lynn.

Nell's major worry was what would happen to Joey in the event of a gas attack. True, gas masks had been issued to all civilians, including the famous "Mickey Mouse Mask," but nothing had been done for pets.

Alf's laughing suggestion of a small paper bag with eye holes met with a glare from Nell. She had promised her son that Joey would be waiting for him when he finally came home.

Mrs. Rumple (whose 30-year-old son had been taken away by police after being caught giving sex lessons to children on the roof of the building) passed away peacefully in her sleep. Her neighbours stood silently by as she was carried from her flat and into the hearse. Alf Smith, the undertaker, gave her a decent send-off, and the few wreaths about the coffin were a welcome splash of colour in the dreary wartime setting.

Although many in Britain were feeling the effects of the gasoline rationing, in Nell's area petrol was of little concern since no one owned a car. Most people walked or used public transport to get around.

With the threat of invasion, the ringing of church bells was forbidden. They were to be rung only to warn of an invasion.

The threat also brought with it a popular image of a Britain filled with spies. Posters warned the population of the danger of loose talk. "Be like Dad, keep Mum" screamed from walls everywhere.

The press churned out stories of Germans and Italians who, although Britain had been their home for many years, were by their very accents suspect.

Responding to this surge of hysteria, Churchill issued orders for foreigners living in London to be rounded up. Police arrested 15,000 classed as Grade C. Ironically, many were Jews who had escaped the horrors of Nazi death camps and were only too anxious to fight the hated Hun. Some were brilliant scientists who could have played an important role in the war effort. Instead, with thousands of others, they were hustled to converted English holiday camps on the coast.

Some, like Renée Ascher, who was fortunate enough to escape from Europe with her mother just before the outbreak of the war, found their reception far from what they had expected:

I CAME TO ENGLAND with my mother as Jewish refugees from Vienna, Austria, just two months prior to the outbreak of the war. I came from an upper-middle-class, loving and protected, family background.

As a consequence of the happenings at that time, and being hunted like an animal by the Nazis, my dad's only way out had been to commit suicide the day after my twelfth birthday on June 18, 1938.

I had been placed in an Austrian orphanage while my mother worked as a volunteer nurse at the Jewish hospital, relentlessly writing abroad for help to escape to England and be free from oppression.

We found a sponsor who placed me in a boarding school in a coastal area of England. My mother — who had never had a paying job in her life before — was to be the matron, and since we couldn't speak English, she communicated with the head-mistress in French. However, being an "alien," my mother was soon forced to leave here and go to London to find employment, so we couldn't stay together.

Eventually Renée joined her mother in London:

MY MOTHER was asked to send me to Canada. While wrestling with the problem of coming to a decision, she had a dream about children's heads bobbing in the sea; their mouths were open and she threw bread to them. When she told this vivid dream to a friend, the friend said, "Don't send her."

In fact, the boat I would have sailed on was torpedoed and all the children perished.

Many classed as "undesirable" were deported to the colonies. Known supporters of the Nazi movement were classified as Grade A risks and imprisoned. Among these was Sir Oswald Mosley, the British Nazi leader.

Nell had good reason to feel pleased at hearing the news of his arrest. He had been a frequent visitor to the East End, searching for sympathizers among the poor. Once Nell had been forced to take cover in a doorway as police on horseback battled with Mosley and his followers along the borough's High Street.

On May 31 the government decided to make it almost impossible for spies to find their way around the British Isles. It became an offence to leave a car unlocked or a cycle unattended. All signposts that gave the names of villages and towns, and store signs that gave the slightest hint of their location, were removed. Many felt that the scheme was so successful that only someone with a good map, such as a spy, had any hope of knowing where he was.

Nell and Alf received a letter that their son had arrived safely at his new home in a village in south Wales. His "family" was the kindly village smithy's, and he was enjoying life there. Many children were not so lucky. Time and again Nell heard of parents in the area who had decided to bring their unhappy children home.

4

STRATEGY

ACROSS THE CHANNEL Hitler was facing a unique problem.

With a stretch of water now separating him from the remaining force of the enemy, he had time to take a breath and ponder his next move. France was beaten and all that remained of the Allies were the British, a nation of people that in many ways had distinct ties with the Germans, linked as they were through the blood of royalty.

Did he really need the headache of attacking this island force and in winning, as he surely would, find himself occupying a strip of land that had no visible attachment to the continent? A country whose empire would no doubt continue to harass him from all corners of the globe?

The midsummer sun filtered through the trees of the Black Forest. A slight rustle of leaves and an occasional breaking of a twig as a nearby guard stepped briefly into view were the only sounds to interrupt the thoughts of the fuehrer.

Now that he was back at his headquarters near Freudenstadt he had time to think. He had every reason to be satisfied with the way the war was going. France had been brought to heel faster than even he had thought possible, yet he was uneasy. Each day he had waited in vain for the message that the British had seen the light, recognized how hopeless their situation had become and were ready to talk peace. So why were they continuing to hold out?

Hitler returned to Berlin and continued to wait. A month after the fall of France, he was finally convinced that the fat old English man with the cigar was determined to continue the fight.

Hitler had never intended to attack Britain. He was, in fact, astonished that the tiny island continued to feel that they had a beef with Germany. The original cause of the war, Poland, had been resolved, had it not?

But Winston Churchill and the British people feared that Hitler had in store for their country a German army of occupation, and if the treatment of those who already found themselves under the heel of the Nazi boot was any indication, a far worse fate awaited them. No, Poland was no longer the issue. He, the despised Adolph Hitler, was.

Unaware of this fact, Hitler felt that it was time to make a direct appeal to the British people. On July 19, 1940, Hitler summoned the Reichstag, and with Goering and 12 of his field marshals to spur him on, he delivered an appeal to the good sense of the island race across the Channel:

IT ALMOST CAUSES me pain to think that I should have been selected by fate to deal the final blow to the structure that these men have already set tottering. Mr. Churchill ought perhaps, for once, to believe me when I prophesy that a great empire will be destroyed — an empire which it was never my intention to destroy or even to harm.

Yet three days before he delivered that speech Hitler had issued a directive for the invasion of Britain.

At the end of the speech Goering and the others gave their fuehrer the customary standing ovation. The chief of the Luftwaffe had reason to cheer. He had been promoted to *Reichsmarschall* and was confident that with the new rank anything was possible. If only the fuehrer would give him the honour of sweeping clean the skies over Britain with his beloved Luftwaffe. Then Hitler could float his armada across the Channel under a sky no longer protected by the Royal Air Force.

By the first of August Hitler made a decision. Goering would have his way. After he destroyed the RAF, the invasion from the sea, code-named Sea Lion, would take place.

When Churchill heard the news he was not impressed. Any attempt at an invasion "would be suicidal." Much more troubling was the thought of the Luftwaffe's massive bombing attacks, which had proved so successful in Poland.

Unlike the German army and navy, the Luftwaffe was a new service full of daring young men eager to establish themselves as the modern knights of the air. There was only one question: they had yet to meet an opponent who could put them on their backs; if and when that happened, could they get up again? For the Luftwaffe had been used only to support ground troops. In the coming battle they would be an army with wings, the first force to set off into enemy territory without the assistance of an advancing army.

The British forces were just as unsure. Since this was to be the first time an army with wings had been used to fight a battle, they were in the dark as to what kind of defensive action to take.

Generals on the ground could study historical battles in the hope that they wouldn't repeat the mistakes made by the likes of Napoleon. Air-force leaders had no such advantage. As they pored over their maps, they had to devise methods of attack and defence for which there were no precedents.

Royal Air Force commanders fought long and hard against the thinking of the older, military ground forces and finally won acceptance for the kind of battle they were prepared to fight.

British Air Chief Marshal Sir Hugh Dowding's advantage was that he knew exactly what Goering had in mind. Dowding's strategy was to hold out long enough for help to arrive in the form of enough aircraft from factories assembling them as quickly as possible and pilots from training schools to wear down the German air machine. The Luftwaffe's target would not be shivering civilians and beaten troops cowering in trenches and ruins of flattened cities. No, the British force would be leaping into the air to meet the enemy — an enemy far from home, and over hostile territory with unreliable weather conditions.

Goering's forces were champing at the bit. Just a few minutes away was a tiny island packed shoulder to shoulder with crazy people who figured they could hold out against the greatest air power the world had ever seen.

His plan was simple. First the Luftwaffe would attack the airfields in the south of England. Once these were unusable for British fighter planes, he would turn his attention to the remaining RAF bases in the north of England.

He thought he would need four weeks.

For Nell and her friends in the East End, all the signs pointed to the dreaded bombing of their area. Alf Smith, the undertaker, was particularly worried. How would he cope with the inevitable large numbers of dead? And his 24-year-old son had been called into the services despite Alf's strong request that he be exempt.

In Britain, as the threat of an invasion grew, young and old alike jumped into action. Government departments struggled to keep up with the mounds of confusing information being released and advice being given. *The Daily Express* suggested that in the event of an invasion people should leave the area. On the same day, *The Evening Standard* advised people to stay put.

Although intelligence reports convinced Churchill that the chances of an invasion by sea were remote, he decided to keep his feelings to himself. He believed that if the civilian population thought the enemy was about to land on their shores, this having their backs to the wall, so to speak, would fill them with a greater sense of danger. If, on the other hand, they felt there was little danger of an invasion, why would they care what was going on across the Channel? History has shown that a people defending their own turf produce a much more effective fighting force.

It was decided to organize a civilian army consisting of those unacceptable for full-time military service. Anthony Eden, the newly appointed minister of Defence, made a plea on BBC radio suggesting that such a force could play a major role in holding off an invading force. This new army was originally called the Local Defence Volunteers, but was quickly changed by Winston Churchill. With his ability to turn a phrase, he called it the Home Guard.

The Home Guard quickly swelled to a force of a quarter of a million men, which was an incredible show of loyalty, especially since the work was without pay. Pat Millet lived in London and was one of those who joined the Home Guard while it was still called the Local Defence Volunteers:

AT THE TIME we irreverently called them Look, Duck and Vanish. After signing up we were mustered and formed into columns of three. A uniformed officer counted us off into companies, then platoons, and finally into sections consisting of six men. I was the sixth and immediately made a corporal, a rank I still held when we finally disbanded. With this honour went a rifle and six rounds of ammunition — one for each of us, I presumed, in the case of dire emergency. An army greatcoat and a tin hat, with instructions to report to platoon HQ where, under a lieutenant, we were to operate signals as soon as the warning was sounded.

Within a short while of being "fell out" the warning sounded. Off I went as instructed only to find at platoon HQ no officer or platoon sergeant. So, as senior NCO, I felt it was my duty to take over first guard.

I dutifully stationed myself in the at-ease position at the entrance to the HQ. Within minutes large numbers of enemy aircraft were seen approaching.

The sound of guns was heard and then I got the fright of my life. From the enemy aircraft there appeared to be many, many white envelopes unfolding. Christ! I thought, Bloody para-chutists — hundreds of the buggers. I was just getting ready to sound the alarm when an old sweat in my section who had been in the First World War appeared beside me and, looking up into the sky, commented on the ack-ack bursts.

Never having heard a gun fired in anger or seen a shell burst, I had mistaken them for parachutes unfolding.

Since the main purpose of the Home Guard was to repel a ground attack that never came, it would seem that this remarkable civilian army served no real purpose. Yet for the individuals involved it did. They were given the opportunity to feel that they, too, were "doing their bit" to defend their country.

Barrage balloons were now over most areas and more numerous than pigeons as they floated back and forth waiting for the first aircraft to entangle itself in their cable webs. Millions of sandbags had been placed against various structures to give reinforcement, and ARP "pillboxes" — concrete gun emplacements — were sprouting like mushrooms throughout the country. These were manned by volunteers who for months had practised what to do at the first sign of enemy aircraft.

E. L. Dimmock decided against attending evening classes at Southampton University College and began spending three nights a week at the Civic Centre on duty as a "spotter" in the underground ARP headquarters:

> IN THE CASE of an incident I would plot on the map where the bomb had fallen and what services were there by little coloured flags.
>
> I had been practising this for several months before war broke out and had also attended first-aid classes, been taught to distinguish between the various gases, taken gas masks around to a good many houses, learned to tape windows with sticky-paper strips, learned how to deal with incendiary bombs with some sand and a long-handled shovel, and how to make a room gas-proof.
>
> In London many cabs were now an ugly grey, having been splashed with paint before being recruited into the Auxiliary Fire Service. Advice was pouring from the radio, and sheets of paper fluttered through every letterbox, telling how to protect oneself against the coming air raids.
>
> From the air the blackout had now closed Britain effectively after dark for the duration of the war. If any German intended to land without a permit he had better be sure he carried with him a damn good flashlight.

Audrey Sara found herself on Mutley Plain near Plymouth after dark, and with the blackout now in effect was having problems finding her way:

> THERE WAS NO MOON or stars. I might well have been down a coal mine. I had to walk about one and a half miles to my home, and after bumping into trees, lampposts and falling off curbs, I asked a lady if she could tell me exactly where I was. Her answer was "Hold my arm, dear. I'm blind and do this walk every day."
>
> She knew every lamppost, tree and curb, and she got me to my home in no time at all.

The beaches were now impossible to cross without becoming entangled in barbed wire, and the British resolve to fight was growing stronger.

Led by an eloquent cigar-chomping man, Britons, like the Germans, had been spurred on by words to see this war through to the bitter end — and win it.

The warm summer haze hung over the Channel, obscuring the view from both sides. Luftwaffe pilots lay around their new airfields in France, Belgium, Holland and Norway, watching gasoline and ammunition arriving from Germany.

Some took an occasional flight to view the small green island across the pond that separated them, and found themselves wondering how it was possible for the inhabitants to feel they could possibly stand up to the might of the German air force.

Most of them were unaware that the two sides were not as mismatched as most people imagined. Germany was not in a position to blacken the skies with bombers. In the pre-war years Britain had shown an ability to build its air force into a fighting machine unlike any the Luftwaffe had faced.

Yet the outcome of the battle would depend on the decisions of two men. In the British corner, Hugh Dowding; in the German corner, Hermann Goering.

Dowding was a widower, who lived with his sister in a house close to his office. A tall, thin and frail-looking 54-year-old, he had served as a pilot in the First World War. By 1934 he had become a member of the Air Council for research and development. After studying the armament of two new fighter planes, he realized that both could be improved by increasing their weaponry from four to eight guns. It was a decision that would have a dramatic effect when the battle finally took place. The Hurricane and Spitfire would be Dowding's leading stars. Impatient and abrasive, he insisted on quality. Once he demanded a change in materials for the cockpits, saying that if Chicago gangsters could have bullet-proof glass for their cars, surely his fighter pilots should be allowed the same protection.

Goering was a large, ribald figure who fancied colourful uniforms, but his clownlike appearance and jovial personality concealed a sharp and active mind. Like Dowding, Goering had also seen action in the First World War. He had, in fact, been one of Germany's most famous air aces, succeeding Richthofen as leader of the legendary Flying Circus.

Now he would have a new aircraft to lead, with one set of wings, not two, and infinitely faster. The Messerschmitt 109, with a top speed of about 355 mph, was as fast as the Spitfire and faster than the Hurricane. It could outclimb and outdive them both and its armament was heavier. True, its range was short and the plane was less manoeuvrable, but with a skilled Luftwaffe pilot at the controls this would not present a problem.

The remainder of Goering's aircraft were slow and ill-equipped for the coming battle, with flaws that had been completely overlooked thanks to the weak opposition encountered in previous combat. But that was not to be their only problem.

In Britain a group of dedicated men in lab coats were developing a complex radar system that would leave the gallant Luftwaffe pilots ruthlessly exposed.

Led by H. E. Wimperis, director of scientific research at the Air Ministry, a group of scientists and engineers assembled in 1934 to figure out how to locate a hostile bomber intent on attacking Britain. From the original meeting a committee was formed. But unlike most government committees, this one moved with incredible speed.

It took just one get-together to agree that a method of detecting approaching aircraft by use of radio signals should be explored and that Sir Robert Watson Watt, superintendent of the Radio Department of the National Physical Laboratory, should be the explorer.

On February 12, 1935, Watson Watt informed the committee that he had developed a means of aiming radio waves that would bounce off the metal parts of aircraft and reflect back to a recorder.

Within weeks he was ready to demonstrate. As a plane flew between Daventry and Wolverhampton, Watson Watt and his group aimed a 50-metre radio beam and stared at an oscillograph. If the line on the graph deviated by as much as an inch, they knew that the plane had pierced the beam.

By the end of March 1935, "radio direction finding" equipment was being assembled from Southampton to the river Tyne.

The value of this radar is impossible to measure. With it, Britain had found a new means of knowing exactly where the enemy was; moreover, it was a device that made it possible for their own fighter pilots to report clearly their positions to a control station on the ground.

It was a defence that was second to none. Although the Luftwaffe had been experimenting along the same lines they were far from perfecting the idea. Their strengths lay elsewhere — in the experience of their pilots and their advanced tactics of aerial combat, honed by recent action in Spain and Poland.

Had the Germans begun the battle before the end of June 1940, they would have been facing a largely untried fighter defence with less than 500 Spitfires and Hurricanes, only half of which were stationed in southeast England.

When the last Hurricanes had left France on June 21, Fighter Command was scraping the bottom of the barrel to find replacements for the 450 fighters and 430 pilots lost in the previous six weeks. Every squadron needed building back up to strength. Before the end of June one-third of them had yet to be fitted with the device that would allow them to be distinguished from enemy aircraft on the radar screen.

Many of the higher-ups in the German military were under the illusion that the Luftwaffe was invincible. The forewarned, concentrated defence they were about to meet over Britain would leave them floundering.

5

THE BATTLE
OF BRITAIN
BEGINS

IT WAS PROBABLY the first battle to be named before it started. On June 18, 1940, three weeks before it did, Winston Churchill rallied the people with "I expect that the Battle of Britain is about to begin."

For Hitler it was a time of indecision. Should the Luftwaffe be acting in a military role, weakening the enemy defences, or should the attack be a political move, hitting the civilian population with a repeat of the bombing attacks that had proved so successful in the collapse of morale in Warsaw and Rotterdam?

The British strategy was easier to define: destroy as many of the enemy fleet as possible but keep a fleet in reserve to tackle the enemy if and when it invaded.

To protect this reserve, Hugh Dowding, now Chief of Fighter Command, secretly planned to withdraw many of his squadrons to the north of London if the southern bases should be too heavily damaged. One area of concern was the civilian population. How would it react to the heavy bombing from the German aircraft that were bound to get through?

Then there were the pilots themselves. For most of them it would be the first time they had seen action.

Many were like "Skeets" Ogilvie and had enlisted overseas. Skeets would later become a squadron leader, but in August 1939 he was a 20-year-old Canadian anxious to get to England:

THE RAF were taking anybody they could get their hands on. I think about 60 percent of pilots were from the Commonwealth — a lot of them Canadians. I got called up on the Monday, had the medical on Wednesday and sailed on Friday.

In the First World War, BBC commentator Charles Gardner had stood on the cliffs of Dover and reported the life-and-death action of aerial combat. He'd made it sound like a cricket match:

THERE'S ONE coming down in flames. There somebody's hit a German...and he's coming down completely out of control.... There's a long streak of smoke.... Ah, the man's bailed out by parachute...the pilot's bailed out by parachute...he's a Junkers 87 and he's going to slap into the sea and there he goes...sma-a-ash.... Oh boy, I've never seen anything so good as this.... The RAF fighters have really got these boys taped....

The myth that aerial combat was a clean, chivalrous fight between two hanky-waving rivals had to be dispelled. The reality was that this was not a game and was no place for gentlemen. The winners would be those pilots able to catch the enemy from behind and shoot him in the back.

The Polish and Czech pilots had learned the lesson that all's fair in war the hard way. Skeets Ogilvie remembered one Polish pilot who flew with him:

HE TOLD US how his friends in Poland had been machine-gunned in the air after parachuting out of their planes. I remember saying to him one day, "But you wouldn't shoot a German pilot coming down in a parachute, would you?" He said, "Well, er, if no one was looking...."

One Polish squadron was so anxious to get into action that it broke off a training exercise to shoot down a Dornier they happened to see.

Ronald Kellett, a London stockbroker who led the squadron explained:

"THE TROUBLE with commanding them [the Poles] was holding them back. They'd have rammed German planes if I'd let them. Time and again I had to tell them that one Pole for one German was not a good enough bargain."

Later, at the height of the battle, Kellett received this message from headquarters:

THE GROUP COMMANDER appreciates the offensive spirit that carried two Polish pilots over the French coast in pursuit of the enemy today. This practice is not sound or economical now that there is such good shooting within sight of London.

So, despite efforts to inject a killer instinct into the flyers, the idea of aerial fighting as a sport persisted.

Many on the ground felt the same way. Betty Martin was an evacuee who'd come back to London:

WHEN I ARRIVED at the station at Gravesend there was an air raid on at the time, and I went straight to the nearest shelter without going home. During the Battle of Britain I had a whale of a time. As I was a teenager, my parents kept shouting to me, "Come down into the shelter! But we were up cheering our heads off at the fighting overhead. To me it was just...fun! We'd get on our bikes and go to where we thought the bombs had fallen and search for bits of the bombs.

For Nell and her neighbours the war was far from a game. Doll's husband, Howard, received his sailing orders and was soon off to join the Eighth Army in North Africa. Nell's other daughter, Nan, now married to John, said goodbye to her new husband, who, although he was still stationed in Britain, was never sure when he would be called to serve overseas.

For the young Luftwaffe pilots scrambling through the heat of August skies, the innocent look of green and peaceful England was deceiving. They soon realized that the equally young RAF pilots in their Hurricanes and Spitfires were gazing on the same scene and scrambling to defend it at all costs. The young Germans were faced with a further problem: the aerial combat was over enemy territory, and their main concern was having sufficient fuel to get their single-seater aircraft back home. But the most damaging weapon they faced was an invisible one: radar.

As the German pilots lifted their wheels and turned toward England they were unaware that "plotters" on the ground across the Channel had already locked them into a radio signal and were following their every move.

Margaret Woolrich was 18 when she joined the air force and headed for Harrowgate to be trained in top secret:

IT ALL SEEMED very secret and exciting. You were trained on a large table with a map worked out in grids, and you were given a grid reference over the telephone. You had little magnetic arrows and you had a long rod with a magnetic head. You picked up these arrows with this rod and put them down on the correct grid reference. So you had this little trail of arrows, one lot for enemy aircraft and one lot for friendly aircraft. As I look back on it, it seems very simple, but at the time we were terrified of failing this test.

You got very nifty with these rods and eventually you could flick your wrist, throw them into the air and then catch them on the rod. You got prouder of doing this than you did of the actual plotting.

I was posted to Kenley Aerodrome. I didn't know then, but the plotters were a fairly privileged group. Because you did shifts and the work you did was very secret, you were excused from most parades and could come in at odd times for meals, so we weren't terribly popular with the rest of the WAAF (Women's Auxiliary Air Force). Also a lot of quite aristocratic people found themselves plotting. The unpopularity of the trade was pointed out fairly forcibly my first night at Kenley.

I arrived in a raid in September 1940 to find a whole group of people under the table in the mess hall. Somebody grabbed me and pulled me under the table where we all huddled. Eventually one of them said, "What's your trade, luv?" and I said, "I'm a plotter." They said, "A plotter! Well, if you are one of them toffee-nosed tarts, you can get out of here," and they pushed me out to take my luck.

When I got there, the ops room had been bombed out recently and they were operating in a butcher's shop in Caterham. We would be bused there. I don't know who it deceived because a whole group of uniformed people walking into a butcher's shop must have looked a bit suspicious.

This was just an emergency ops room, and after just a few months we were moved into a much smarter one in an old rectory, and that's where I spent the war.

It had been pointed out during our training that you only had to put an arrow in the wrong place and that could mean someone's life. So you did feel very bowed down by all this.

It was a very peculiar sort of existence for an 18-year-old, because the boy I went out with one night might be dead the next. We had one girl who always seemed to have fairly swift courtships with pilots who then got shot down. Three fiancés ended up in the same POW camp, by which time there was a fourth on the books, I expect.

The plotting worked this way: one person manned headphones that were connected to radar stations on the south coast. That person gave you plots coming in over the sea. That's where you picked up most of the enemy raids. The observer corps posts around the country gave you plots from seeing or hearing enemy planes coming over. We wore earphones, and when we heard the pilots we placed our arrows in the appropriate positions.

It was terribly exciting. You felt you were at the hub of everything. The people you dealt with were in the newspapers every day. The pilots had the sort of status that pop stars have now. You would get the list of pilots going off on an operation, so you would know if your friend was flying, and then you wouldn't know until they'd all come back and been briefed who was missing.

Goering set about the destruction of Britain's Fighter Command with gusto, attacking airfields at Hawkinge, Lympne and Manston in the hope of, if not trapping them on the ground, making it extremely difficult for them to take off and land.

For those working in the area these raids could be unsettling. Many of the factories set up a spotting system of their own.

T. P. Dean was employed by a company in Maidstone, Kent, and spent most of his time watching the Battle of Britain from the top of a tower:

WE HAD BINOCULARS and kept watch, two of us, and pressed an alarm button to get the workers to the shelters as the planes got close. The reason for this was to keep production going as long as possible.

A heavy attack was taking place on Detling Aerodrome, and I was in my bedroom at home and watching the planes as they bombed the drome. One plane left the scene and headed toward Maidstone. I leaned out of the window to get a better look at whatever this aircraft was, and as he got closer I saw it was a Junkers 87 and that he still had bombs slung, and even as I saw the iron cross on the wings he pulled the release and the bombs started to fall.

In my panic I started to dash away from the window — except for one thing. My braces were hooked on the window catch, and I got about four feet away before I was pulled up short. By the time I had unhooked the braces the bombs had gone off about 250 yards away. The window shook but did not shatter. Lucky for me.

Being young and eager, I dashed round to Marsham Street, Maidstone, where the bombs had landed. Two had exploded and a house was destroyed. Two killed and a few injured. I soon found out that another two bombs had landed in Ashley Street and had not exploded. This is where Paddy came on the scene.

Paddy was a private in the Royal Engineer bomb-disposal team stationed in Union Street. He was sent by his sergeant to check the two bombs that had landed, and then he took matters into his own hands.

One bomb was only a 50-kilo and had penetrated only to the fin, so Paddy decided to deal with it himself. He dug the bomb out in about half an hour, and Paddy, who was a massive man with hands like shovels, picked that bomb out and decided to carry it to the Union Street depot, which was about 200 yards away.

He sweated up the road with the bomb. About 50 yards from the depot there was a pub called the Rifle Volunteer, a pub that is still there. The landlord at the time was a Mr. Whitley, a veteran of the First World War. Paddy was getting tired and gently lowered the bomb to the pavement and went into the bar to ask the landlord for a pint. The landlord, who by now knew what was outside, said, "Paddy, you can have all the beer you want, but take that bloody bomb to the depot first." So Paddy obliged and delivered the bomb to the depot before coming back for his well-earned pint.

In 1940, 20-year-old Marie Lewis was living on England's south coast, where she was witness to many stirring aerial battles:

ONE EVENING I was standing beside our wired and sandbagged shores and saw our planes doing battle over the sea to keep the enemy at bay. The odds were so much against them. When they returned, they rolled over and over, doing a victory roll.

I know they couldn't see or hear me, but I clapped my hands and with tears steaming down my face I called out, "God bless you. Well done, boys!"

The stories of German pilots flying low overhead were many. Violet Phillips was on the golf course when a German bomber crashed nearby:

SO MANY LOCAL PEOPLE were killed rushing over to get souvenirs when the plane exploded. The German pilot was buried in the tiny churchyard of St. Paulinus, in Crayford, Kent. He was buried at the far end of the churchyard with a tiny wooden cross away from all the others.

Marjorie Ulph (now Davidson) was living in an old railway-goods wagon to get away from the air raids, and she arrived home to find her mother jumping with excitement:

"GUESS WHAT," she said. "A German pilot complete with swastika flew low over the adjoining field and the pilot waved to all the people."

The feeling that loved ones would soon be in danger prompted many to change their routines. Nell's husband, Alf, and his brother, Steve, got into the habit of visiting their mother on Sundays to take her out for a drink. Grannie Wicks was now in her 90s, and although she always had a spare bottle of gin hidden in the chimney, she was never one to miss an opportunity to visit the Drum and Monkey.

By the end of the first week in August, airfields throughout France, the Low Countries and Norway were throbbing with some 3500 planes anxious to take to the air and deliver the final blow against the stubborn British.

The Royal Air Force had built a force of 720 operational Spitfires and Hurricanes, but they had one great remaining need: fully trained pilots.

It was estimated that it took 50 times as long to train a Spitfire pilot than it did to build the plane. A Spitfire with a dozen bullet holes in it could be quickly repaired and sent back into the sky. A bullet-ridden pilot was not so easily put back together. Even men without physical wounds were scarred by nervous exhaustion. They needed rest between raids, but instead were climbing back into the cockpits and living on their nerves.

At 21, Bobby Oxspring thought of himself as a veteran:

YOU HAD TO BE ABLE to fly without thinking about it. It's — what shall I say — like playing the piano. You can't be a musician while you still have to look for the keys. And about the end of August, we were starting to get these boys as replacements who hadn't really finished their training. They still had to think about flying the aircraft. And it was pathetic, terrible, to see them go down right away, in their first fight sometimes. You just didn't have to brood on that sort of thing, or let the others brood on it, either.

Bruno Petrenko is now a retired Canadian businessman. In 1939 he volunteered for training as a German fighter pilot. At 22 he was trained on the ME-109 and on August 31, 1940, reported to his first unit — in Calais, France:

I WAS NOT SUPPOSED to be in on the flight over England because I was a beginner. But the pilot scheduled suddenly had stomach pains and had to rush to the toilet.

Everybody was waiting fo him to come out, but he didn't, so they said, "Well, you had better take his place." I was on the mission by chance.

Our orders before we took off were very simple: protect the bombers. There were many units of bombers going across the Channel, and we were supposed to stay above the bombers — not get involved in dogfights. The theory was that British fighters would attack from a great height, they would first have to become involved with us. The orders were "Don't chase British fighters. Just stay above the bombers."

We took off and I followed the squadron leader out over the Channel. It was beautiful weather. The sun was shining and the whole sky was full of planes. A tremendous thick cloud of German planes, and you couldn't see the beginning and you couldn't see the end.

There was anti-aircraft fire near the coast. You could see the white puffs against the blue sky. Sometimes you would feel the effect of one of the puffs when it got too close to you. The plane would jerk or jump.

As we continued on you could see here and there burning aircraft suddenly diving out of control. Sometimes a parachute would blossom out of the plane, its white showing up against the blue of the sky. But as a fighter pilot you don't have time to enjoy such things. You have to be very careful and keep watching the sky above and behind you, because this is where you expect to find enemy fighters. After a while there was an attack in my area. We were at a great altitude and I noticed someone behind me. He scored some hits on my plane but luckily hit the protective shield at my back.

It was the first time I had experienced this — it was a kind of ticky, ticky, tick — but it made me feel good that the shield had protected me. Anyway, I evaded whoever was firing at me by nosediving. Then I climbed again, trying to catch up with my unit. I remember thinking, Well, this isn't so bad, but suddenly I was again attacked from behind. It was so fast that I couldn't evade it before it came — at least, as a beginner I couldn't. As I went into a dive I thought, Well, what do I do now?

Some pilots said that in such a case you go down to tree-top level and go home, but I thought that sounded too easy, so I decided to climb again — which was a big mistake. An experienced pilot would not have made it.

I was attacked from below and to the right — where there was no protective armour.

The glass from the cockpit splintered, the instrument panel splattered and now I was really hit — many times. I blacked out.

When I came to I was in a vertical dive. I noticed lots of noise, a kind of fluid coming from the side of the plane, and the ground approaching very fast. I realized I had to catch the plane immediately and get it out of the dive. I did, and in doing so, blood rushed from my head and I blacked out again. When I came to I found I was at tree-top level with little power left in the machine. I had to find somewhere to land.

I looked around and saw two Spitfires behind me. They were shooting at me occasionally, but I guess it was difficult because I was going so slow and was not flying in a straight line. Anyway, I saw an English parklike landscape with some bushes and trees. There was a group of trees ahead of me and I said to myself, What I have to do is to try to get enough speed by flying directly at the trees and then hope I have enough speed to jump over them and then go down. I did this and then blacked out once more.

Petrenko was found by John Clancy, a British sergeant, who was out with a searchlight unit:

I WAS STATIONED between Brentwood and Epping in Essex and was driving around when I heard that there had been a German aircraft shot down in the area.

I jumped into my van with a couple of men and took off. We soon located the aircraft a few hundred yards from the Brook farmhouse. It was on its back, nose well into the ground (actually the nose had broken away and was 90 yards away and still burning).

The tail was cocked up in the air with the plane lying at a 45-degree angle. The airscrew had bounced about 200 yards away. The wings had broken off.

On approaching, I could see the pilot hanging upside down in the cockpit, bleeding and unconscious. The hood of the cockpit was shattered.

I set out at first with my rifle breathing fire and slaughter, but when I saw this poor gory head hanging there, the rifle went to the ground and I started to wriggle my way under the plane to get the victim out. After a rather hairy time flat on my back underneath the plane, I finally got him out. With the aid of some water from the van I tried to bring him round and clean up his face.

He seemed to have head injuries. The first thing he said was "Spitfire?" I said, "Yes!" Then he said, "Why are you being so good to me?" This stumped me and I came back with a rather fatuous reply. "I don't know. You might have been one of our boys, mightn't you?" Then he looked up at me and said, "How far to the sea?" To which I could only reply, "Too far!"

Petrenko, the Messerschmitt pilot, was taken to St. Margaret's Hospital in Epping:

I WAS THERE for 10 days. There was always a British soldier with me making sure I didn't escape. The nurses and everyone were very kind.

After 10 days I was ready to go and my head was dressed with an impressive bandage like a turban. I put on my uniform and a young British officer and soldier took me by train to London. On that trip the names of all the stations we passed through were Bovril. I didn't know then that they had removed the names and left the advertisement.

We left the station in London and got into a car to go to a POW collecting camp near Hyde Park. On the railway trip I had managed to talk to the British officer — my English wasn't very good — and we discussed history and things. Anyway, in the car he suddenly said, "By the way, have you ever seen Buckingham Palace?" and I said no. He said, "Well, would you like to see it?" and I said, "That would be terrific!" And then he leaned forward to the driver and told him to go by Buckingham Palace. We drove up to the gates and it was around the time of the changing of the guard. We sat there and watched. It was a wonderful and warm gesture.

If Bruno Petrenko had been able to continue with his London tour he would have found that life in the city was moving along much the same as it had in peacetime.

Princess Margaret had once again had a birthday picture released, her tenth, and the theatres were open once more. You could see a revival of *The Chocolate Soldier* or really hit it big at the Hippodrome, where you could see Winston Churchill watching his son-in-law, comedian Vic Oliver, perform. You would be able to sing along with Vic, who had found that his audiences were only too ready to forget what was going on outside and belt out the songs of the day.

Nell tried to take her mind off the war by returning to her old habit of visiting the Trinity movie house on Sunday evenings. After escaping in the dark with Ronald Coleman for a couple of hours, she was ready once again for the struggle to put together a decent meal for Alf with the meagre rations the government allowed. Maybe a visit to the cat-meat shop was the answer. For two pence it was possible to get some horse meat. Alf had eaten it in the First World War and said it wasn't bad. Just a little sweet tasting.

As to vegetables, the buff-coloured identity card allowed six ounces of vegetables a day for each person, but thanks to the generosity of Fanny Price and her husband, who ran the greengrocer round the corner, this could easily be more.

The straits between Dover and Calais had become such a hotbed of enemy activity that the British decided to withdraw the destroyers sitting in the harbour. Convoys making their way through the narrow straits were to do so only after dark.

The crew of the first of these convoys, some two dozen coal ships, were assembled in a Southend dance hall and told that from now on their orders would be given by the Admiralty. The Germans claimed that they controlled the Channel, but this coal convoy was going to prove them wrong. It was a matter of prestige.

Unfortunately the Germans heard it all on their radio devices on the cliffs of France. As the convoy manoeuvred itself out at dawn, a group of German torpedo boats came out of the half light and sank three of the ships. As the day progressed the dive bombers attacked out of a low-ceiling cloud. Some of the ships carried barrage balloons that held the dive bombers at bay. But at midday a large force of Luftwaffe fighters escorted dive bombers over the target. Four merchant ships were sunk and a further three badly damaged.

The remaining ships scattered and attempted to reassemble off the Isle of Wight only to find 82 JU-87s with an escort of fighters ready to finish them off. Only four of the original 20 ships made it to Dorset. Few of the survivors were rescued, because the British had no air-sea rescue organization. A German pilot down in the water had the benefit of flares, sea dye, yellow scull-caps and one-man dinghies, and the chance of being spotted from the air by the many float planes that were part of their search-and-rescue program.

Tubby Mayne, 39, had the extraordinary distinction of having enlisted in the First World War and seeing action again (most pilots were in the 18 to 20 age bracket). He was flying a Spitfire when the German air force began to make its attacks on the Channel convoys:

CONVOY ESCORT duty wasn't so bad when you could find the convoy. But there were bad days, even in that fine summer, and looking for ships in low cloud and rain, and damned great waves, green ones, just below you, well, all you could think of was your Mae West. Do you know, we were supposed to wait until we were in the drink and then unscrew the nozzle and blow the thing up with our own lungs, and then screw it up again.

It's fantastic to think how primitive our equipment was. After all, the whole battle was fought with rifle-calibre bullets. But the Spitfire and the Merlin engine — they were superb. They were what gave us confidence. You got in that cockpit and shut the canopy and you felt you were in a fortress and no one could get at you.

For Goering it was time to begin day and night bombing of the British air industry to ensure that the aircraft he was so decisively crushing would not be replaced. The operation, code named *Alder Tag* (Eagle Day), was to begin August 10. However, before they made the opening moves, the British early-warning radar systems had to be put out of action.

Fleets of Stukas, Dorniers and Heinkel bombers protected by ME-109 fighters roared across the cliffs of Dover to attack the installations dotting the coastal areas of England. The huge masts of the radio receivers made an easy target, and the opening raids damaged four stations and destroyed another.

Once again the British pilots threw themselves at the raiders, and despite the fact most were flying in shirt sleeves, they were bathed in sweat.

Goering decided to cancel future attacks against the early-warning system. Rather, he favoured a massive attack against the airfields and gave the order for 1485 aircraft to take to the air on August 13. A report of bad weather convinced him to postpone the attack, and he gave orders for the planes to be recalled. However, many of the planes were already on their way and did not receive the order to return. The fighters who did get the message made their way back to base, leaving the bombers undefended.

By midafternoon the weather had improved and once again Goering's planes set off across the Channel to attack the fighter airfields on the south coast. The chosen targets were thought to include 11 fighter stations, but in fact only one was a fighter station — and it was missed by the raiding bombers. But by late afternoon a fighter unit successfully lured a group of Spitfires away from a planned bombing attack on Detling Aerodrome. Sixty-seven British airmen lost their lives during the attack, and 22 aircraft were destroyed on the ground. It had been an eventful day, and in some areas of the country, nightfall brought no let-up. The Nuffield Spitfire factory was suddenly paying host to a group of German bombers that flew in under cover of darkness. They scored a bull's-eye with 211 high-explosive bombs.

At last it was possible to take a tally for the day. Forty-six German aircraft had been shot down at a loss of 13 RAF planes. Forty-seven fighter planes had been destroyed on the ground. It had been costly for both sides.

The weather cleared on the morning of August 15, and Goering decided to launch a massive attack. Nearly 1800 sorties involving 500 bombers made their way to a 500-mile stretch of the English coast.

The radar was waiting for them. Huddled in five closely guarded huts along the south coast of England, the women had worked tirelessly at their top-secret apparatus, marking for destruction enemy aircraft long before they reached the cliffs of Dover.

Calmly and deliberately they recorded the progression of V-shaped blips and, after sifting and assessing each mark, delivered long transmuted streams of data to the eagerly awaiting fighter pilots. Even as the German planes lifted into the air above France, phones were already ringing warnings to the British fighter stations and anti-aircraft posts.

The little-used Lympne airfield caught the first shower of bombs. Hangars burst into flames, workshops fell apart, and dirt and debris rose into the air from an almost deserted runway.

Overhead, planes wove their white vapour trails above the fields of Kent. Occasionally a puff of smoke would become a glow of flame and the nose of an aircraft would dip and begin to slowly spiral toward the ground. Sometimes the white canopy of an escaping pilot's parachute could also be seen swinging back and forth.

Observers on the roof of a Maidstone church in the heart of Kent cheered wildly as a German aircraft burst into flames. They were about to ring the church bell, when someone realized that this was to be done only to signal an invasion.

The German aircraft based in Norway made their one and only major daylight attack without the protection of a fighter escort. They were slaughtered on the long flight home.

One hundred other Luftwaffe planes made their way from the north to the Thames estuary. The British 11 Group tackled them over Folkestone and Deal. Two to three hundred more German aircraft crossed Hampshire and Dorset.

In the north, 100 Heinkels and seven ME-110s were spotted approaching the Firth of Forth. Sunderland sirens warned of the coming raid, and by the time the all-clear was sounded, 24 houses lay in ruins.

As the day wore on the fierce battles raged high in the sky, and all that could be seen were the wind-blown smoke trails of dogfights.

The women at their radar tubes followed the fleeing planes, Spitfires and Hurricanes in hot pursuit, checking not only their course but their speed and elevation. Suddenly they noticed the tell-tale blips of a new formation of German fighters waiting to ambush the pursuing British fighters as they approached the Pas de Calais. The British fighters were immediately ordered to break off the chase and return to base to rest and refuel.

Back in 11 Group's underground headquarters on the outskirts of London it was time for an assessment — good. And a cup of tea — well deserved. But the battle had only just begun. Before it was over a lot more blood would be spilled over the green fields of England. The battle for air supremacy was creeping closer to London. Croydon airport, an obvious military target just to London's southeast, was attacked. A great deal of damage was done to the airfield itself and the surrounding houses and factories.

Mollie Fairey was a nurse at the Croydon General Hospital. Her mother was a district maternity nurse. She remembers the morning her mother was out visiting mothers and their babies:

MANY MOTHERS had their babies at home in those days. At 1 P.M. Mum got home for lunch. By 2 P.M. she was dead with the house bombed to pieces. I knew nothing of this at the time as we were very busy in the hospital.

I went home for my Monday off-duty, 9 to 12 A.M., and found my house completely flattened.

I was 19 years old and didn't know what I should do, but eventually went to the police station.

My mother wasn't found for three days and then the funeral service had to be rushed through as there was an unexploded bomb in the churchyard.

Jean Gough (now Ager) lived at Wallington, Surrey, close to Croydon airport:

I WORKED at a chemists in High Street, and one evening at about five o'clock some fighters came over doing the victory roll (which they often did). My boss and I and others were watching from the shop doorway when there were loud explosions. (It was said afterward that the German pilots had followed our fighter pilots back.)

My boss, who was an auxiliary fireman, grabbed his tin hat and made for the fire station, telling me to go opposite to the air-raid shelter in the corn chandler's cellar. When I arrived there the elderly owner asked me to wait whilst he got the straw out of the cellar (he sold rabbits). He would sweep it out.

Meanwhile, a bus pulled up and its driver asked if I wanted a lift. When I arrived home my mother said that my dad, who was a stretcher bearer in the ARP, had gone to the airport to see if he could help. (Over 300 people were killed at Bourjois perfume factory alone.)

When my father arrived back in the early hours of dawn he said that relations and friends of the people trapped and killed were so frantic to get to the casualties they hindered the ARP, and firemen had to train their hoses on them so they could get on with their job.

Ethel Sumbler was cycling home at Purley Roundabout when a large fleet of bombers approached the town:

NOBODY TOOK any notice as we were used to seeing large formations of planes, as Croydon was the home of London Airport at the time.

Everyone thought the approaching aircraft were ours. The planes turned over my head toward the airport, and when I looked again they had released their bombs, falling just like rain. In blind panic I jumped off my cycle and ran, everyone else doing the same. Windows were falling out and buildings were crumbling and dust was thick all around us.

People were just leaving work and were caught out, not being able to get to any shelters. Sixty-three people were killed, and 45 seriously injured. Many more were slightly injured. Many of the dead were buried in a mass grave as they were unidentified.

The raid was all over in 15 minutes, and it was not until some time after the last bomb was dropped that the alert sounded. The reason given for the delay was mistaken judgement on the part of officers operating the system.

Some of us did get to a shelter when it was all over and I fainted away with shock. But I was grateful to be alive.

The Spitfires and Hurricanes were a shock to the Luftwaffe flyers, who were under the impression that the RAF was seriously short of planes and pilots. A battered German force made its way to its airfields in France. The Englishwomen working over the large maps and boards in the operation rooms began to push the discs representing German aircraft slowly toward the east. Elderly civilian observers on the coast lowered their binoculars and prepared to make their way back to nearby villages. There would be an incredible story of British victory to tell that night at the pub. In Churchill's words, the RAF had "cut to rags and tatters separate waves of murderous assault upon the civil population of their native land."

It was an important victory for Britain and had a deeply demoralizing effect on the Luftwaffe bomber pilots.

The early-morning mist over northern France had cooled most of the airfields, and as the pilots made their way to their Heinkels and Dorniers they pulled up the collars of their flying suits. The climb carried them up away from the villages and peasants that they had tried so hard to befriend. Candy for the children and promises that the war would soon end had produced some change, but whether this was the defeated French people's acceptance of them as human beings or the realization that life must go on, they did not know.

But there were other things to occupy the pilots' minds as they climbed into the clouds. Once again they were about to cross the battlefield of the day before, and once again, the Hurricanes and Spitfires would be waiting.

6

THE BATTLE IN THE SKIES

NELL LEANED OUT the window to bring Joey in for his daily bird-cage clean, and got a terrible shock. The canary was gone. "The pigeons probably 'ad 'im fer breakfast," said Alf.

To Nell it was no joke. "Is that wot yer goin' ta tell young Ben when 'e comes 'ome?"

St. George's Buildings echoed with the sounds of the many children whose parents had brought them back from their "adventure" in the country. But Nell and Alf had not followed suit. They were convinced that all hell was about to break loose and it was just a matter of time before Hitler decided to attack London. Sitting in his favourite chair by the window, Alf read aloud from The Evening Standard, *which suggested that all lampposts should be torn down. In London alone there were 100,000 of little or no use. "Makes sense," said Alf. "Fink of all the guns that lot could make." Nell looked up the courtyard at the familiar lamppost. Her mind was not on guns but on her son and his mates who used it as a makeshift maypole.*

August 16 saw no let-up in the pressure. Another 1700 German aircraft came at Britain like a swarm of bees. Two JU-88 bombers dived out of a low overcast sky and scored direct hits on the hangars at Brize Norton, southwest of London. All 46 aircraft housed there were destroyed.

There were incredible acts of heroism on both sides during these remarkable days. Flight Lieutenant J. B. Nicholson, of 249th Fighter Squadron, was the first member of a Fighter Command to be awarded the Victoria Cross. He was flying a Hurricane, and as he weaved and bobbed in the middle of dozens of enemy aircraft his plane was struck by four cannon shells. He was wounded, and his petrol tank, which had been hit, began to pour flames into his cockpit. He was about to bail out when he saw an ME-110. He immediately climbed back into the burning cockpit, got the German in his sights and fired a cone of rounds into the fighter. Only then did Nicholson, burned and bloodied, parachute from his plane. As his feet touched the ground an overly excited Home Guardsman shot him in the rear end.

For the next three days the skies over Britain were criss-crossed with the white tails of zooming planes as the Luftwaffe attacked the fighter bases.

Bombs scarred the fields, and many of the returning British fighter pilots found themselves skidding on the craters that dotted their home bases.

Skeets Ogilvie, now a Spitfire pilot, reported back to his squadron and found a hell of a mess:

WHEN I GOT to the station, Middle Wallop, the Germans had plastered the aerodrome a few days before and blown up a hangar. A big door had come down on two little guys running for their lives and this goddamn steel door came down, and they became part of the tarmac.

By August 18 the battle had truly begun to turn in favour of the British. Almost a quarter of the German bomber strength was made up of the slow-moving Stuka dive bombers, which had more than met their match in the faster Spitfires and Hurricanes. Alarmed at the Stuka casualty rate, Goering first increased their fighter escort, then withdrew them completely from the battle.

Meanwhile, the British pilots who'd survived were red-eyed and exhausted, and the bombed factories had not been able to replace the lost Hurricanes and Spitfires.

Pilots were soon being transferred from the Fleet Air Arm and Bomber Command to Fighter Command.

The training course for flyers had been cut back drastically; a pilot now had only two weeks between learning to fly and going into combat. And in the high stakes of aerial warfare there was much to learn.

On August 24 large-scale Luftwaffe raids started again. Goering leaned across his large map table and thumped it with his fist. "We have reached the decisive period of the air war against England."

The Luftwaffe lifted its wings and returned to the battle with a thousand planes a day flying high above the green fields of England. Day after day the women in the radar huts pushed the markers across the boards and tracked the planes as they crossed the Channel. The voice of the ground controller calmly directing the young British pilots was interrupted time and again by the cry of "Tally-ho!" as the RAF pilots made contact with their German counterparts.

As August staggered into its last week the damage was beginning to tell. Thirty-three major attacks had been made, 23 of them against airfields and nerve centres of Fighter Command. In two weeks the Germans lost 373 planes and the British 277.

Both sides continued to deceive themselves by exaggerating the number of "kills." The bigger the air battle, the greater the claims of numbers of those shot down.

Those watching from below were equally sure that smoke flowing from a retreating enemy aircraft would overcome the pilot and force him into the sea. Every Spitfire appeared to be executing a victory roll as it made its way back to base.

Parachutes were a common sight — and the target of any members of the Home Guard who were in the area. One German pilot now living in Canada remembers watching them from the air after bailing out:

I WAS SWINGING down in my parachute in a tricky wind and bleeding from a head wound. I looked down and laughed uproariously at the antics of the British Home Guard down below. They had their eyes on me and were constantly falling in ditches as they ran this way and that....

Luftwaffe pilot Friedrich von Goetz was shot down by Spitfires over Dover when flying an ME-109. He remembers the precise time it happened:

IT WAS EXACTLY 10:23 A.M. because by some reflex action I looked at my watch when my chute opened. Spilling air from my chute, I managed to avoid a high-tension wire and hit the ground hard. The Home Guard quickly grabbed me. One gave me a cigarette, one began to bandage my head and another started to strangle me.

From the Vatican to the United States feelers were being sent out in the hope of bringing Germany and Britain together to discuss terms.

The population gritted their teeth and looked to "Winnie" for guidance. Churchill was determined to carry on to victory and secretly wished for increased bombing, culminating with an attack on London itself. Only then could he silence any talk of peace and give himself a reason to attack Berlin. (Although the RAF had been bombing Germany since the invasion of the Low Countries, as yet no attack had been made on the German capital.)

But Hitler was aware of what Churchill wanted and did his utmost to guard against any action that would gain for his opponent the sympathy of an isolationist America. He strictly forbade any attacks on London and was quite content to have Goering concentrate on British airfields.

Despite the incredible courage and the distinct successes of British fighter pilots, the action was beginning to take its toll on them. Those who had not been shot down were exhausted. Many were flying three or four sorties a day. Repairing a plane was difficult, but replacing pilots as fast was impossible. Churchill raced around the countryside in an air-force uniform giving encouragement at the various fighter stations and radio speeches proclaiming, "We would rather see London laid in ruins and ashes than that it should be tamely and abjectly enslaved."

On the night of August 24 fate intervened. Six German bomber pilots left their bases for a night raid on England. As the bomb aimer in the leading plane crawled into position, he glanced down and watched the coastline of England slide slowly by. Ahead small puffs of anti-aircraft fire pricked the night sky.

A thick cloud cover over the target area left him and his fellow crews staring into a soft white pillow. His fingers gripped the bomb release and his thumb slowly depressed the button to release his bombs on the outer edge of London as he had been ordered. They landed on the centre of the city. Churchill ordered immediate reprisals against Berlin.

One hundred British bombers headed for the target. Not surprisingly, the raid, which was planned in such haste, was not a success. Of the 80 bombers sent to bomb Berlin fewer than 30 found the target. The following days brought four more raids, and although they were largely ineffectual, the raid on the night of August 28 killed the first German civilians.

This infuriated Hitler, who had promised his people such a thing would never happen. He immediately issued orders for massive retaliation raids on British cities. No longer would Goering be pointing at tiny British airfields and fighter bases. Now his pudgy finger would point at major cities — and ultimately, when his fuehrer gave the word — at one of the biggest targets in the world.

While he planned his attack on London, Goering decided that bombing raids on other cities would encourage Britain to quit. After a series of night raids on Liverpool and Birkenhead by 157 bombers, pilots claimed that the raids had been concentrated and weighty. In fact the bombs had fallen over a wide area, and damage to the ports themselves was slight.

Amy Crighton was living in Wallasey, near Liverpool:

THERE WAS just my husband and our two-year-old son. We had a little knitted hat for the boy and I stitched some pads to put over the ears so that he could sleep through the bombing. Going down the shelter was all routine for us. My husband's job would be to get dressed and grab the baby, and I would take the baby's bottle and a candle — there were no lights or anything in the shelter. We would keep all the clothes and other things in the kitchen by the back door all ready to take each night. I always remember one night we went down and my husband had put his pants on back to front. We didn't used to wait for the warning. We just used to watch for the searchlights, and when they came on my hubby would say, "Get ready. We're going to get it tonight."

One time in the early evening I decided to take the baby and go for a walk with my husband's sister. We went down to visit my auntie, and the searchlights came on and the warning sounded and she said, "Oh, you're not going to get home tonight." They lived in a small two-up and two-down and used the brick shelter in the middle of the road. Anyway, we joined her for the night. Next morning we went back to the house and saw my husband. He'd been on the night shift and was on his bike looking for us. When we got home the door was off and the army was in the house and garden, and we weren't allowed in. A time bomb had fallen and was buried in the garden. Funny thing was, the mailman had been, and since he couldn't get in he'd thrown the letters up the hall, and in that mail were my husband's calling-up papers.

Doug Higgins and his family were the only ones on his street who had put in an Anderson shelter. When the bombs began to fall on Merseyside, they suddenly found themselves with plenty of company:

HAVE YOU EVER seen a whole roadful of people trying to get into one air-raid shelter?

Then there was old Mr. Brown across the road who liked his pint from the hotel up the hill. He came home one dark and moonless night. A bomb dropped and a Belisha beacon [a light standard at a pedestrian street crossing] chased him down the hill. Those little legs never went so fast in their life.

He fell into the shelter that night exhausted!

How to become a teetotaller overnight!

Attacks on London seemed increasingly likely; yet more and more people were leaving their gas masks at home. Alf and Nell were no exception. On hearing the ARP suggest that they keep the masks by them at all times, both of them had great difficulty remembering where they had placed them for safekeeping. Propaganda announcements were suggesting that germs sprayed from the air were the newest Nazi weapon. Alf merely commented that with all the germs already in the building, a few of Hitler's wouldn't make much difference.

In preparation for the attack on London, Goering decided to destroy the fighter stations that would be called on to defend the capital. Croyden was first on the list.

E. C. Williams, who was living in Croydon, suddenly found herself grabbing everything she could and heading for the back garden:

ONE SUNDAY LUNCHTIME in September 1940 the largest bombing raid over Croydon took place. I rushed my daughter, 18 months, and son, two and a half, into the Anderson shelter at the bottom of the garden. I rushed back to my kitchen, grabbed my hat and the roast leg of lamb and rushed back down the shelter.

In 1939, one woman, who joined the ambulance service in Croyden as a voluntary driver, tells how she felt:

I HAD JUST come off duty at sunset, and from a bedroom window saw several planes come in very fast and low, then saw the "black eggs" dropping. I shouted to my husband. We watched the smoke rising until it almost concealed the sunset. After about five minutes the sirens sounded, but of course the planes had long since sped off. The factory that had been hit had been working nonstop with girl staff, no warning had been given, and the results were indescribable. Some of the stretcher bearers and rescue men were physically ill. Later on I was always relieved that I was a driver and had to wait outside until a casualty was brought out.

Although the daylight raids were frightening, many watched the action taking place overhead. This diversion was not possible after dark, and then there was only the sense of danger. Pamela Fife was on duty on the four-to-midnight shift in the main control centre of the Croydon ARP:

THE SIREN had not been sounded, we were quietly chatting, and all but three of the girls in the report centre adjoining our room were either in the canteen or the restroom.

At 7:30 all the lights went out, there was indescribable noise, objects flying in all directions, choking dust, then a few seconds of complete and utter silence before cries of help could be heard. Our roof spotter rang down to us, and although I don't remember, I was told that I answered him, and when informed that he thought the police station opposite had been bombed, I gave him the reply — that it was us!

The staircase down to the basement was blocked with debris, so we had to get out via the underground passage leading to the police station. The three girls in the control room were killed (if the siren had sounded, the death toll would have been higher). Apparently a lone German plane had jettisoned just two bombs, one hitting us and the other the Working Man's Club, where there were a great many killed.

I had head and facial cuts, and on arriving there I was horrified to hear a voice saying I would have to have my head shaved. I was being married in two weeks!

Patricia Brooks was 11 and living with her family at their home near Croydon. There was a small room under the stairs that her mother was convinced was the safest place to be in an air raid:

WHEN THE SIREN sounded my father called us from our beds, complete with blanket and pillow each, to settle in for the night. An older sister, who had a small baby, would never respond, and my father would keep shouting until she did, hugging the baby. We were all very dopey from lack of sleep, and one night when this happened it was ages before we realized that my sister was hugging and talking quietly to a pillow, and Terry, her small son, was lying on the floor in the bedroom.

Mrs. Famfield was evacuated to Brighton as a 13-year-old, but she returned to her home in Croydon in 1940:

WE WERE at the Davies Theatre watching a film when a bomb landed about six rows in front of us. Luckily it was an unexploded bomb. There was no panic due mainly to some soldiers who were in the audience keeping everyone calm.

I used to visit an auntie with two small babies trying to run her life in London's dockland and the devastation was terrible. The rats had all been disturbed and were running along the clothesline in the kitchen where the nappies were drying.

When the British still didn't see the light, Hitler decided to issue the order for sea-invasion preparations to begin. The plans were dropped into the lap of Field Marshal von Rundstedt. Embarking from the various seaports between the estuaries of the Scheldt and Seine, the sea armada was to make its way to the southeast coast of England between Folkestone and Brighton. At the same time an airborne army would drop and capture the cliffs of Dover. He figured that securing the beach-head would take about four days; then the main advance inland would begin to take the high land from the Thames estuary to Portsmouth. London would then be cut off from the west — and only too anxious to throw in the towel.

A back-up operation would transport army units from Cherbourg up the Severn estuary on 3000 barges, tugs and motorboats. The possibility that the Royal Navy, still the strongest in the world, would not take kindly to an operation of this kind convinced Nazi high command that air supremacy was vital. Therefore, much of the immediate action was left in the hands of Goering, who convinced Hitler to plan the invasion for the middle of September. Goering assured the fuehrer that while he was clearing the skies of the Royal Air Force, he would be quite happy to take on the Royal Navy at the same time.

Goering decided to begin with an attack on British shipping in the Channel. It was a clever move calculated to lure the British fighters out to defend their ships. This would weaken them before the Luftwaffe launched its big attack.

Dowding was quick to warn the Air Ministry and Admiralty that to protect the shipping in the Channel he would have to commit a large force of his fighter aircraft — force that would be needed at a later date.

By the end of the first week in July, German attacks on shipping in the Channel established a pattern that would continue for four weeks: relatively small groups of German aircraft, never more than 50 at a time, forced Fighter Command into battles off the coast where radar could give them only the shortest of warnings. The German fighters and bombers could quickly get into formation above the radio network, and five minutes after take-off they could be across the Channel; the Spitfires took 15 minutes to reach them. More and more British ships were sunk as the Luftwaffe increased their attacks on the Channel convoys. Those living in a coastal area such as Dover had front-row seats. George Betts tells what it was like:

MY BROTHER AND I were standing beside some tunnels at the foot of the cliffs when without warning two Messerschmitts that had been converted to carry one bomb each, swooped down over our heads and loosed the bombs at the huge naval-supply ship, the *Sandhurst*, that was moored quite close to us. It had a destroyer named the *Codrington* alongside her, being refuelled.

All at once all hell broke loose, and me and Colin, picking ourselves up after the blast had knocked us down, were nearly knocked down again as workmen and sailors ran into our tunnel. Afterward we found that the supply ship was on fire and the destroyer had been almost broken in two alongside her. The navy managed to tow the crippled *Codrington* away, but she was hit by bombs as she made her way into the Thames estuary and was sunk.

The Thurbins along the landing decided to move. Although they were not going far it was a blow to Nell, as the two families had known each other for many years. The sounds of Barty, Billy and

Patty running up and down the balcony would be missed. The Thurbins found a flat that was just a 10-minute walk from St. George's Buildings and promised to keep in touch. They did not. The poor never do.

Dowding was under increased pressure to move his fighter force closer to the coastal areas where the ships could be protected, although he knew his force needed the distance and time to build up their numbers to match the German forces.

Unaware of the success that the British were having with their radar, the Luftwaffe began sending lone aircraft out over the North Sea to gather weather information and take photographs of future target areas.

Still, all-out battle had yet to be declared. Both sides used the time to build up their strength.

A dynamic Canadian industrialist, Lord Beaverbrook, was given the task of rebuilding Britain's aircraft fleet. As the new minister of Aircraft Production, he set about the task with a vengeance, turning out Hurricanes and Spitfires at the rate of 500 a month, four times the number of Messerschmitt 109s the Germans were able to produce in the same period.

Although success buoyed the spirits of most, those actually doing the work were exhausted, and output sagged. A concerned Ernest Bevan, minister of Labour, reduced the maximum working hours to 60 hours a week to protect the workers from burn-out.

Lord Beaverbrook proved he was fallible by introducing a ridiculous campaign called "Saucepans into Spitfires." Everyone was asked to donate their saucepans for the war effort. Unfortunately, only when millions of them had piled up did some bright spark realize that they were useless. Saucepans contain insufficient aluminum for the making of a fighter aircraft.

Nell didn't send any saucepans. Her family had little enough in the kitchen as it was without sending them off for someone to bang into a Spitfire. Besides, what with the rationing and all she was too busy looking for a decent meal to cook for Alf. Once, she bought some live eels at the market and was bringing them home on the tram when the brown paper bag broke and they went wriggling all over the floor. When she'd gathered them up and got them home, Alf refused to eat them, anyway.

Many on the home front had always been unhappy about what they felt were injustices. The feeling that there was one law for the rich and one for the poor changed after Dunkirk. Everyone felt they had their backs to the wall, and "all for one and one for all" now seemed to be the order of the day.

In the countryside women from every social stratum were forming small groups in order to teach themselves how to handle small arms. Leaflets poured from government offices suggesting how cars could be easily immobilized, leaving any invading German out of luck. The Home Guard had now experienced weeks of regular drills and were confident that any German Panzer unit would be making a great mistake if it hoped to advance in their neck of the woods.

Nevertheless, it was a success from the boys in battle that the country needed.

Alf Smith, the undertaker, had problems of his own. Aside from the difficulty of getting help to replace his son, London was full of military traffic making its way to the coast. Alf's beautiful Belgian horses were constantly shying from the shouts and yells of the passing troops. One lorry driver, who had cut him off in full procession, was stupid enough to stop when Alf flagged him down. The undertaker promptly left the grieving family and marched boldly up to the driver. Lifting his rolled umbrella, he took aim through the window and hit the driver in the eye. Alf Smith was taken to court but released on his promise of good behaviour during future funerals.

7

THE GERMANS ARE COMING

FORCED TO STAY IN BRITAIN for the summer holidays, many made their way to the coastal towns in the south. They discovered that despite the strands of barbed wire winding their way across the sands to defend the country against the threatened invasion, there was one thing that would never change: the sea breeze — there was still plenty of that to be found. There were places, however, that remained unattractive to the holiday-maker. A holiday at Dover could result in injuries from the German shelling that began on August 21 because of their newly acquired bases around Calais.

The sound of these guns, which could be heard quite clearly across the Channel, was the only noise coming out of Europe.

Valerie Street had gone to the south coast of England to visit her fiancé:

I WAS 18 and engaged to a lieutenant in the Royal Marines, and he had invited me down for a weekend in Portsmouth. Little did I know then that I would be caught in my first enemy blitz.

Bill had found me some digs with Mrs. Jones, a landlady who was well known to the Marines as kind and clean, and one who provided good wholesome food.

The first night there, Bill and I had just finished supper when the tummy-tightening wail of the sirens sounded. Bill had to leave hurriedly to organize the manning of the in-shore guns at the marine base.

Within a few minutes the booming of heavy guns could be heard, followed by the crump of landing bombs. For a while the earth seemed to shake and tremble, and the noise outside was quite deafening. To my surprise and consternation, Mrs. Jones began to panic and started shouting and calling out to God to save us all. Her screams each time a bomb landed somewhere were frightening, and never having been in a blitz before, I felt an urge to get out of the house and take my chances where I could see what was going on, however danger- ous such a need was.

Mrs. Jones tried to drag me into the cupboard under the stairs, but I was very averse to such a claustrophobic atmosphere and I tried to tell her, above the noise from outside and her screams of panic from inside, that I was going to stand outside in the garden.

Grabbing a saucepan from the kitchen, I put it on my head as protection from falling glass and debris and hurried outside.

There was a cacophony of sound, and a brilliant array of colours lit the sky. I wondered with frightening awe what on earth was happening to Bill, as I heard the sickening thud and crump of falling bombs, coupled with the shrieks of terror emit- ted by Mrs. Jones indoors.

Suddenly, as I stood watching and listening, there was an almighty explosion, and glass from the two front rooms came flying out into the garden and the curtains billowed out, completely in tatters. My heart stood still for a moment and I really thought I had gone deaf. With the now whimpering Mrs. Jones indoors and the ever increasing noise and bombs and bumps and wardens' whistles and shouts from up the road, I felt totally inadequate and helpless. My conscience told me to go back indoors to see if I could calm poor Mrs. Jones.

When she saw me with one of her saucepans on my head she suddenly started to laugh. The awful tension was broken.

I went into the kitchen to make one of our endless cups of tea and sat for a few moments with Mrs. Jones until she felt calmer and the noise outside lessened. The big naval guns continued to boom and whistles could be heard blasting away farther up the road, but we eventually heard, thank God, the sound of the all-clear.

After a couple of hours of waiting and wondering and worrying, Bill turned up. We threw ourselves into each other's arms with relief and happiness.

The battle in the sky affected other areas of Britain, too. M. Fitzgerald was picking hops in Kent when a fighter plane came out of the sky with smoke trailing from its tail:

MYSELF AND THREE other young lads jumped up across the railway lines, then across some more fields, and as we were running towards the plane which was burning, I picked up a machine gun. It was hot and covered in oil. The lads said, "Keep it as a souvenir." I said no and threw it toward the plane.

The pilot parachuted down and went toward an orchard. The local policeman lived nearby. He was a very tall man — six foot seven. He was on his bike and asked us where the pilot had dropped down. I pointed to where I had last seen him, and he said, "Let's go and have a look." We crossed some fields and into the orchard. We saw him standing by a tree with his parachute caught up in the tree. He put his hands in the air. He was a nice lad, blond. The policeman said, "Come on, lad," and took him away.

Nell, who by now had made a regular habit of "Sunday night at the movies," extended her evening's entertainment by meeting Alf at the Red Lion on her way home. Spirits were hard to come by, but as most of the locals drank beer, there was little complaining about the lack of Scotch. The supplies of beer were not as regular as during peace-time, and when they did come into the pub, they were usually moved to the saloon bar. It was not long before Nell and Alf had promoted themselves to the "posh side."

Many, like Esme Temple, got their entertainment at home:

I REMEMBER in particular the radio, and when it snapped, crackled and popped too much to listen to because of the raids, it was turned off and we all sang.

Those not singing in their homes or in theatres were probably singing in the local pub or shelter. Singsongs were becoming wildly popular, for they made life a little more bearable.

Talk of what it would be like to be occupied by the Germans was in short supply, and most people in the pubs restricted their conversation to the chances of being hit by a bomb "wiv yer number on it."

The first of September was a Sunday, but no day of rest. The war was almost one year old and at long last appeared to be creeping toward London. For those keeping score of the battle in the air it was not good news. Fourteen German aircraft had been shot down to the British loss of 15. On the second of the month, the score was little better — 35 to 31 — and on the third, 16 to 16.

The Germans were trying a new tactic — mixing the fighters in with the bombers. It seemed to work, as the planes made 33 successful raids on England's airfields from August 29 to September 7.

On the ground, people continued to stare at the sky and watch fascinated as the swirling vapour trails twisted and turned above their heads.

Despite the losses, some people, like Leon Kay, found the sight of high-flying aircraft a thing of beauty:

I WAS IN THE GARDEN of our new Luton home with my foster mother when she exclaimed, "Aren't they beautiful!" pointing to some silver-coloured planes flying high in the clear blue sky. A series of violent explosions followed and we discovered later that the planes were German.

The exaggerated counts of the numbers of German aircraft being destroyed had convinced everyone that the Royal Air Force was invincible and that if an invasion was around the corner the same courage that had allowed "the few" to throw the Luftwaffe from the sky would toss the Germans into the sea.

On September 4, after British bomber attacks on Germany, Hitler made another of his threatening, furious speeches: "If they attack our cities, we will rub out their cities from the map! The hour will come when one of us two will break and it will not be Nazi Germany!"

As the people in the shelters chorused "A Nightingale Sang in Berkeley Square," bombing by daylight continued. But Fighter Command had come a long way from the opening days of the Battle of Britain and were determined that the Luftwaffe would not repeat the successes of earlier attacks.

Air Vice Marshal Park brought his squadrons forward to tackle German bombers heading for London over Dover and Beachy Head. He was able to divert them and force them to drop their bombs on Canterbury.

The summer was almost over and the weather was beginning to change. Constantly told that the British were almost out of planes, one German pilot on seeing a huge RAF formation, remarked sarcastically, "Here they come. The last 50 Spitfires."

For Nell life in St. George's Buildings had changed very little. She still looked through the window every evening at five o'clock to see Alf coming home from work, though looking out was not as easy since Alf had criss-crossed the window with tape.

One evening Nell was anxious to tell Alf that their downstairs neighbour had been sentenced for stealing a quarter pound of tea from the docks where he worked. The magistrate had given him six months in prison, telling him that she was determined to stamp out this kind of petty thieving in the docks, and then adding, "Don't you know there's a war on?"

Servicemen on leave could be seen everywhere and seemed to spend most of their time in dance halls with local girls, who were dancing to relax after long hours spent doing their bit in the war-time factories. "If this is war," one 17-year-old was heard to say, "why am I enjoying it so much?"

Sid Shilton was living at Walthamstow, in northwest London, and decided to join the Auxiliary Fire Service.

I'LL TELL YOU why I joined. Two of my mates went to a fire station one night and said it was a really good night out. They give you some drills and a bit of instruction, then we go out and have a few pints afterwards. So I said, "Well, that sounds all right. I'll come up with you tomorrow." We didn't get paid, but when we did our initial training, we got issued with a uniform and all the rest of it, but otherwise there was no money in it. We used to go out occasionally with the regular firemen on their red machines to get some experience, but we just went whenever we felt like it.

In pre-war Britain it had been customary for women to give up their jobs when they married. But once war was declared this labour force was in great demand, as May Powell of Oldham soon realized:

I FOUND A JOB sewing and making babies' gas masks. Each stitch had to be perfect, and when you finished the sewing you had to let the sewing needle finish in the last four stitches.

Most women at the factory (the poorer ones) had pawned their wedding rings and had replaced them with six-penny ones from Woolworth's.

My brother was manager of a pawnbroker's shop and he bought second-hand jewlery that had come out of pledge, so I took them to work and sold them to the ladies who wanted to replace their Woolworth ones.

After this job I went to a little fish-and-chip shop, and people used to come into the shop selling their coffee or clothing coupons for a few shillings.

When I became pregnant I was ordered to go to the Labour Exchange and was asked if I deliberately got pregnant so I would not have to go into war work.

The women who did remain at home were learning to use stirrup pumps, which were for putting out small fires caused by incendiary bombs. But for most of the poor, the pump was of little use. It required that users have a tub or bucket large enough to set the pump in, and the poor did not.

A 1939 public-information leaflet explained how to remove an incendiary bomb by placing it on a shovel or in a steel helmet. "Never place the bomb in water." Doing so would cause it to explode.

Despite this frightening information, the incendiary bomb was the easiest type of bomb to deal with; certainly there was little people could do about a high-explosive bomb other than to put as much space between them and the device in the shortest possible time. Incendiary bombs were packed 36 in a cylindrical container. One bomber could carry five containers, which were dropped at a predetermined height and spilled over a wide area, causing considerable damage if left to burn. An incendiary bomb was about a foot long and three inches in diameter. The moment it struck the ground its magnesium core threw off a glittering shower of white, molten splinters in a radius of about 10 feet. It would take about a minute for the shower to end, at which time the bomb would glow, and after 10 minutes burn itself out. The trick was to snuff it out before it caught anything else on fire. A sandbag or shovel of dirt could do the job.

Across the Channel in The Hague, Goering declared that the British had pulled most of their fighter force from the forward fighter stations, and therefore what was needed was an attack that would bring the few remaining Spitfires and Hurricanes back into action.

The target would be London. The attack would force the reserve Spitfires and Hurricanes into combat against a vastly superior force.

This proved to be a major error in judgement, and one that influenced the outcome of the war.

By ceasing their attacks on the exhausted and battered Fighter Command operation rooms and command posts, the Germans gave the British time to recover; just one more week of devastating attacks on the airfields of Fighter Command would have made the defence of London impossible.

Alf came home and told how, along with some of the others at the factory, he had gone onto the roof and watched the dogfights. Although they had been pretty high in the sky, Alf, like most people living in areas of aerial combat, had become an expert on which aircraft was which, and he could certainly tell the difference between a bomber and fighter.

His daughter Doll sat busy reading the latest letter from Howard, who was serving in the Middle East. Although it had obviously been censored heavily she was sure that he was happy and had found a nice quiet section of the war to occupy himself until Christmas, when she was sure the war would be over.

Nan's husband, John, although extremely fit to look at, had been found to have weak eyes and had been transferred to the Pioneer Corps and found himself posted close to London.

Nell began to think how lucky Nan was to have her husband so near. She thought about her young son, living in the small village in Wales with the local smithy. She wondered if this trade might prove useful to her son until Alf reminded her that the only horses needing shoes in the London area were those owned by the undertaker and the bobbies. The thought of his son ending up as a bobby was enough to have him reaching for his Maclean's Stomach Powder, especially since he had just got the news that it was thanks to the police that his mate from downstairs found himself in the "nick."

8

TARGET
LONDON

THE AFTERNOON OF SATURDAY, September 7, 1940, was hot, and many were out in the parks or in their gardens sipping tea. The narrow streets of the East End of London were filled with the mix of people who called the area home. Wages were low, unemployment was still high and the sense of the frustration common to a slum area pervaded. The East End had seen rent strikes and violent clashes between Fascists and Communists as they fought to win over the working class with their promises of a fair world. The Fascist leader, Oswald Mosley, had targeted the area — an odd choice as his message fell on a lot of Jewish ears. The result was to be expected: punched noses and bleeding heads. Mosley claimed that the Jews had grown rich on the backs of the poor; the fact that the East

End of London, home for many Jews, was steeped in grinding poverty seemed to have escaped him.

But on this warm September day all was peaceful, even as the soldiers in nearby Victoria Park polished and overhauled their anti-aircraft guns to have them ready to protect the most congested area in the British Isles.

It was close to five o'clock when Nell heard the first sounds of approaching aircraft. She was in the market close to London Bridge, and her first thought when she looked down the river was that they were friendly planes. Suddenly bombs began to fall. Almost 400 bombers with 600 fighters to protect them had made their way up the Thames and were now dropping their deadly cargo. Within minutes, it seemed, flames were leaping from the docks, as incendiary after incendiary hit its target. The clang of fire engines racing through the streets mingled with the sound of the ack-ack guns that had roared into life with the first sight of the tiny black dots. Nell joined others who were now running to get home. Those too far from their own homes quickly took cover in the brick shelters that stood in the centre of most streets. Smoke was billowing into the streets from the huge fires that engulfed the ships docked at Woolwich, then West Ham.

Nell made her way to the ground-floor level of St. George's Buildings and was sheltering with her two daughters and neighbours under the overhanging landings that jutted from each floor. At the end of the alley they could see fire engines leap into action and head for the docks on the Thames.

Alf, along with most of the men, made his way to the roof of the building to watch the attack. It was a sight he would never forget. He raised a cheer as a squadron of British fighters arrived overhead and a fierce battle began. Each bomb blast rocked the 100-year-old structure, and there were times he felt sure it would collapse, but he was too fascinated to leave the roof and join his family.

Many of the old structures in the city were not so lucky. The buildings surrounding the docks of London were brought down in a cloud of plaster and dust, burying the occupants huddling inside.

George Gardiner was sitting in his garden reading when the warning went:

I DIDN'T TAKE too much notice as there had been many warnings during the Battle of Britain, but no bombs. After a while I became aware of the sound of many aircraft and, jumping up, saw a number of aircraft flying fairly low and in perfect formation.

A couple of anti-aircraft shells burst some way from them. My mother came dashing out of the house and we both dove into the Anderson shelter.

After they had passed we came out and things seemed to go quiet again. (The planes had gone on three or four miles to the docks.) After a couple of hours the all-clear went, so we had tea.

Living on a corner, I was able to peer over the wall and look along the street. I saw what I thought were thunder clouds, but after a while realized it was smoke. I went out and found that a plane had scattered a few incendiaries around on its journey to the docks and that the National Fire Service were putting out the fire in a house around the corner by the simple expedient of knocking a hole in the roof and putting the hose pipe in, which I thought would do more damage than the fire.

Skeets Ogilvie was now a Spitfire pilot at the fighter station in Middle Wallop, which was called upon to assist the overwhelmed London squadrons. It was his first combat mission:

THEY SCRAMBLED our squadron and the old controller was saying, "There's a 100-plus coming in over Dungerness, then 150-plus coming in over Greenay," and after a while I heard the flight commander say, "Tally-ho!" God, my eyeballs were hanging out and I couldn't see a goddamn thing in the sky. . . . I looked all around and still couldn't see any of them . . . and I'm thinking, What's this 100-plus business and I can't see any of them. Then I hear, "Okay, pretty boy, beam attack." I was number four in my section and I followed the others and rolled over. . . . I nearly pooped my pants. . . . The whole German air force was just flying along about 3000 feet below me.

The air was just crawling with these planes with black crosses on them . . . Heinkels and Junkers . . . I'd never seen so many planes in my life.

Down we went in an attack right through the middle of them, trying to decide which guy I was going to try to take a shot at. . . . I went through so fast that I didn't have time to fire my guns. . . . I thought, Holy cow, this is a great start to combat flying. I pulled up on the outside and started climbing back up to get in a position to do an attack by myself. And two ME-109s drifted by just on the inside of me. They were so close I could see the pilots both looking inward, the other way — neither of them had seen me on their outside. So I came out the other side of them and jigged around, got into position as quick as I could, opened fire on the first one and, Christ, I hit the second one . . . didn't hit the first guy I was aiming at at all. Anyway, by now I'd finished all my ammunition and headed back to Middle Wallop, and do you think I could find that airfield? They all looked the same to me in that part of the world. My fuel was going down, and I thought, Oh, God, what a first trip, a belly-landing in a field. Back to Canada and the colonies for me.

Meanwhile in the dockland area in east London, blue-clad fire fighters, atop ladders thrust into the air, ignored the continuing bombing and flying shrapnel and directed channels of water into every impossible-to-control blaze. The heavy-unit pumps could pump as much as 1000 gallons a minute, and with the back-up of smaller pumps, usually towed by taxi-cabs, the London Fire Brigade was an army at the ready, and about to face its greatest test.

Guided by the flames, hundreds of other German aircraft made their way up the Thames. Iain Dick was watching:

THEY FLEW in a circle for protection. I'd see the occasional glint of sun on metal as a fighter dived into the ring, and then slowly pealed away with smoke streaming from him and go into a lazy dive to destruction. The bombers came back at night to take advantage of the flaming docks as an easy way to pinpoint their target.

The ack-ack was in action, of course, but to conceal the desperate shortage of guns, they would fire a few rounds from their positions and then pull up hooks, rush to another spot and bang off a few more rounds.

Unfortunately a 40-mm Bofors gun would sometimes be parked outside our cottage, bang off a few clips of shells before one of the gunners would knock on the door and beg a cup of tea. Alas, the vibration of their gun had usually shaken the cups off the shelf to smash on the floor, so they lost out.

Millie Driscoll remembers Saturday, September 7, well:

AFTER TEA I went with my eldest sister to St. George's Church when the air-raid warning sounded. After a little while we left the church, and whilst walking down St. George's Road for home, we could hear the noise of the planes and gunfire. I wanted to run, but my sister said we would be all right and held my hand very tightly.

When we got to our house in Paster Street, neither of us had a door key. All the family were in the Anderson shelter in the garden and could not hear us ringing the bell and knocking on the door. I was very frightened and crying. Eventually my father came up from the shelter to go to the toilet, and he heard us and opened the door.

We went straight into the shelter, which was very small, meant, I think, for six people, but there were 10 of us in it. Later on my father and a friend went into the house to get some refreshments for us. When they came back he told my mother that we would be lucky if we didn't get hit, as we were surrounded by fire.

I was sitting on a small folding stool in front of my sister with my head on her lap, and I fell asleep. Suddenly I was awake and there was a lot of noise. Everybody was talking and my father was trying to get the door of the shelter open. When he did we couldn't see the house, just a big cloud of dust. As it settled we realized that the house was still there but badly blasted. The back-window frame had come out and was blocking the shelter door. Then we heard whistles and the ARP men were running up and down the street calling everyone to come out, as the gas pipes in the road had fractured and there was danger of further explosions. As we walked into the house, a candle on the kitchen table was still upright and burning although all the windows had blown out and the doors were lying on the floor.

When we got into the street there was a big hole in the road and the gas leak was burning. We had to go to the public shelter under the big Burton's shop at the corner of St. George's Road and London Road. The sky was very bright and we just walked along with our neighbours. I don't think anyone ran.

The next day my father and a friend put up boards at the windows, tidied up as much as they could and fixed the street door on again. We had no water, only a stand pipe on the pavement about five or six houses up from ours, and no gas.

My poor mother had to cook for six of us each day on an open fire for 12 or 15 weeks. We didn't even have a fire with an oven at the side like some of our neighbours.

The people in authority said we could continue living in the house, but we couldn't sleep there because it was too dangerous. So we slept in the public shelter until the Wednesday, but it wasn't very deep. We could hear all the noise. My father had been blown up three times in the First World War and the noise and no sleep was having a bad effect on him. Our doctor said he should get out of London or sleep in the underground, so from then on we slept down the tube. I would go across with my cousin at about four o'clock with an old thick table cover and wait outside the entrance of the Northern Line tube station until the warning went, then run down the spiral emergency stairs onto the platform to claim our place between two chocolate machines. My mother would come as soon as she could with her and my bedding. My father and sisters would arrive with their bundles and we all slept on the platform.

In the morning my father and sisters would go home in time to get ready for work, and my mother and I would wait for the all-clear.

Every morning there was more damage to the house and Dad would try to fix things before going to work and Mum would clear up the dust and soot that seemed to be everywhere.

K. James was a seven-year-old living in the East End of London the day the German bombers came up the Thames:

I HAD TWO PLAYMATES, twin boys, the Hardings, the same age as myself, who lived in Gainsborough Road, the next turning.

We were playing together that day, when my mum called me in for tea. Not long afterward the siren sounded and we went into our Anderson shelter in the garden.

Soon the sound of aircraft could be heard and my dad called me up to see a great mass of planes flying up the Thames. They seemed to darken the sky. Then the bombs started to fall. We crouched in the shelter, which shook with each explosion.

Suddenly a tremendous bang was heard and Dad said, "That's a near one," and after a while the all-clear sounded.

We left the shelter to find windows broken in our house. A bomb had fallen in Gainsborough Road.

The bomb had made a direct hit on the shelter of my twin friends, killing them and the rest of the family — all but one older brother who had been at a wedding in East Ham.

As the day came slowly to an end, the sounds of the bombers faded, but the roar of the burning warehouses continued, and as the red glow from the docks competed with the setting sun, a great cylinder of black smoke curled its way upward. The bombers returned at 8 P.M. and continued with their carnage. The grey dust of humble houses that had crumbled throughout the day was once again stirred and flattened.

Throughout the long night, the Luftwaffe crossed and recrossed the Channel in a slow agonizing procession to the capital as the people of London settled into the shelters for the night.

Violet Regan was a young woman living with her husband in the East End of London:

THE MORNING of September 7 was beautiful. The warm sun shone from a clear blue sky onto the little streets of Cubitt Town, Isle of Dogs. I had premonition of the terrible ordeal to come. Of late the Luftwaffe had made quite a few hit-and-run daylight raids, and when around midday the sirens blared their warnings I did not feel unduly disturbed.

My husband, who was a member of the Poplar Heavy Rescue Service, was off duty and we were about to sit down to lunch, but on hearing more gunfire than usual, we decided to go into the garden and stand for a while outside the Anderson shelter.

Very soon we heard the ominous drone of distant airplanes — German airplanes. The drone rapidly became a roar.

I remember the rising excitement of the neighbours as they anxiously called to each other. The frantic barking of the dogs — and meowing of my cat, who immediately sought shelter of his own choosing. Suddenly there they were. Silhouetted clearly against the blue of the sky. They consisted of three separate formations and they were heading in our direction.

I watched in horror as bombs fell. My husband yelled at me to take cover, then he was off to join his colleagues at the Heavy Rescue Depot in neighbouring Millwall. I helped to calm my terrified neighbour and her three little children, who were screaming with fright, and stayed with them until their father arrived. Then I went into my own shelter.

For a long time I sat listening to the awful bedlam going on outside. To the explosion of bombs, clanging fire bells. During short lulls I heard the crying of terrified children and the voices of agonzied parents trying to soothe them. The barking of hysterical dogs went on and on. There seemed to be no respite from the awful din.

Later on I head someone calling my name. It was our air-raid warden. He said that time bombs had fallen in the vicinity of a nearby oil-storage factory and that the tanks were liable to blow up at any minute. Everyone must take refuge in the Glengall Road School.

I walked to that school carrying one of my neighbour's children wrapped in a blanket. Great canopies of billowing smoke blotted out the sun, and barrage balloons were falling down in flames. We were obliged to slap out sparks that alighted on us from all directions. More and more people were making for the school, and as we walked through this nightmare we could hear the enemy planes above us diving with banshee shrieks to deliver their bomb loads.

When we reached the school, all of us, men women and children, were herded into a long corridor which smelt dankly of damp cement.

I was terribly worried about my mother and father, and it was with great relief I spotted them ahead of me in the crowd. Everybody settled as comfortably as conditions would allow on the cold concrete floor, our backs against the rough surface of the wall. My parents sat opposite me and my sister and her three little ones made up the rest of our family group. Soon there was scarcely room to move. The bedlam outside never ceased.

At long last there came a lull, but with the coming of darkness the Luftwaffe resumed their attacks and all hell broke loose again. They added fuel to the already raging fires and started fresh ones. It was terribly frightening to hear the fierce crackle of flames and constant crashing of falling masonry.

Several times the huge building we were in seemed to rock with the impact of high explosives. Gaping windows were all along the corridor and in my position I was sitting beneath them, facing the wall opposite. Fascinated, I watched the lurid reflection of the flames dancing on the wall. They lit up the corridor and bathed us in a baleful glow.

The menacing drone of the enemy bombers set already taut nerves on edge and somebody screamed, "What's the matter with our guns? They haven't fired a shot!" It was quite true. Apart from the solitary salvo loosed at the beginning of the raid, no gun had fired a shot in our defence.

Thirst was worrying us. Very few had had any drink or food since morning, but water was unobtainable because the mains had burst. I thanked God that my two little girls were safe in the countryside of Oxfordshire.

By some miracle the school escaped the bombing and nobody was hurt. But the awful expectancy had been too much. Overwrought women bust into tears and the little ones, sensing their fear, began to scream.

Something had to be done and done quickly, so with parched throats a few of us of tried to sing.

Then my old dad, possessor of a fine rich tenor voice, began to sing something they all knew — "Just a Song at Twilight." It was touch-and-go at first as he tried to adjust his dry throat. Then here and there a few voices around us joined in, then more, and soon it became a swell as they sang the lovely old refrain with him.

What a tonic that was! Sleep had been denied us and it was such a long, long night.

When at last daylight came and the all-clear finally sounded, there was a collective gasp of sheer relief. In the cold light of morning we looked like scarecrows, smoke-begrimed and filthy; hair awry and clothing badly crumpled.

After sitting in one position for such a long time we ached in every limb, and it was especially difficult for the older people to get to their feet. Very soon the wardens and special police appeared amongst us with their helping hands and comforting voices. "Ups-a-daisy, Ma," and "Come on, old soldier, show a leg there!"

Listening to them and seeing them brought a lump to my throat, because they were in a far worse state than we were.

Misses Foster and Turner were professional dancers about to get ready for the evening performance at the Queens Theatre, in the East End, when the attack came. With the rest of the cast they had fled to a nearby shelter.

WHEN THE ALL-CLEAR finally went we returned to our dressing rooms to pack up our belongings. It was then that the telephone rang.

On answering it, I was astonished to hear someone was wishing to book seats!

A. W. Wall and his wife had taken shelter in a block of offices:

WE DECIDED to go by bus to see if my wife's mother was okay. She was. However, the sirens went off and we dashed back to my mother-in-law's house, which was on a street of old-style four-storey buildings. In the block where we took shelter were about 20 people of various ages. The raid got heavier and heavier. I felt tired and lay down beneath a window. I don't know what time it happened, but there was a terrific crash and a blinding flash. A bomb had fallen through the front of a block opposite. It blew me out of the window and into the street. There were screams, and fires, dust and debris everywhere. I climbed over the debris at the front of the block into the second lot of blown-up sandbags and pulled the first person I saw out into the flame-lit street. This person was covered in dust and grit, as I was. The person was my wife! To think that of all those in there it was my wife I rescued. God was good!

I went in again and helped those who could move out. One of the people I was carrying asked me to put him down by a wall as his leg ached. I looked down. He had lost a foot.

Irene Kent's father had a fruit-and-vegetable shop in Holloway Road, London. The family was fortunate to have a Morrison shelter in the home, but nevertheless felt they needed something extra to protect them:

DAD PILED hundredweight sacks of potatoes on top. We hated any kind of shelter, but my mother was insistent.

We were in (or under) the shelter when we heard a bomb whistling down and a colossal bang. The ground seemed to come up at us. "That's close," said my father, then looked out onto the main road. Grey forms were running past the shop saying, "It's around the corner, guv!"

My father rushed off, for my grandparents lived around the corner in Liverpool Road. It was a direct hit with one of the first 1000-pound bombs.

My granddad, step-grandmother and aunt were killed, but two other relatives were rescued from under the piano.

Daylight finally arrived and with it the sound of the all-clear. Nell and the neighbours made their way slowly back to their flats. The blackened and dishevelled firemen, though exhausted, continued to direct their hoses on the smouldering remains of ruined buildings. The stench of smoke from the burning docks drifted through the streets. Alf quickly put on the kettle and prepared a breakfast for the exhausted group. After spending a short time on the roof watching the action, he had decided to go to bed, sleeping through the ack-ack and falling bombs. The night of terror for most Londoners was just another noisy night for an old infantryman who'd been in the trenches of Flanders.

Through the open window they could hear other Londoners staggering along the glass-strewn streets with their bedding, hoping against hope that their homes were still standing. Many of those houses that weren't lay open on one side like a stage set on which the curtain had lifted before the performers appeared. Others were no more than piles of rubble, here and there a framed photograph showing happier times sticking out between crumbled bricks.

Doll and Nan suggested that they tour the streets to view the damage, but Nell and Alf would have none of it.

Everyone knew there was more to come.

Those who did venture out turned their heads in embarrassment from people who were scrambling over the rubble searching for the prized bits and pieces that made their lives meaningful.

But these were the lucky ones. During the raid, a thousand of their fellow Londoners had been killed. The German planes had dropped about 330 tons of high-explosive bombs and more than a thousand incendiaries. The smoke still rose above the river east of the city.

Eventually London's black taxi-cabs were commandeered for the war effort. With a tow-bar affixed to the back to pull a small pump, a cab would be deployed as a back-up appliance to the main fire-fighting force.

With the main seats in the taxi-cab being taken up by 10 50-foot lengths of canvas hose, the crew had to sit on the little square pull-down seats ordinarily used for extra passengers.

For Churchill, it was almost a magic moment. Placing his hat on the end of his walking cane, he twirled it above his head as he toured the streets and received a hero's welcome from people whose life he had done little to improve. All was forgiven. They were looking to a leader who would avenge the bombing they had survived.

Dickens and Jones, a large department store in Oxford Street in London's West End, became such a favourite for many seeking a deep shelter that police were called for crowd control. People were quickly organized into a queue, and by 7 P.M. on Sunday the first 700 were allowed to take shelter in the large basement. In the months to come thousands more would line up for hours in the hope of getting inside.

R. R. Bennett was 15 when the war started. Living in southwest London, he had seen the gradual build-up to the raids. First the daylight attacks and then sounds of aircraft after dark.

In the second week of September he and his father looked to the night sky and were surprised to find masses of parachute flares falling:

AFTER A YEAR of total blackout, the novelty of night light seemed too good to miss. As I recall there was no bombing, no ack-ack fire, just the sounds of aircraft droning to and fro across the sky.

A few days later R. R. Bennett and his father were told by a passing air-raid warden that what appeared to be a very large bomb had landed in a nearby cemetery:

IT HAD REDUCED the superintendent's three-storey house to bungalow status, but he and his family, all friends of mine, apart from being shaken, bruised and scratched, were otherwise safe. An enormous amount of superficial damage had been done to surrounding property. Our attention then focused on a large parachute hanging on its lines from the brick parapet of Clifford Bridge, adjacent to our house, which carried the South Circular Road over the Waterloo-Richmond railway lines. Our immediate reaction was of course that a parachutist had landed. Without any clear thought of what we were going to do, Dad and I went up onto the bridge to see what it was all about. We saw a large cylindrical canister propped against the parapet; and it was from this that the parachute was dangling.

More rumours of earlier in the day came to mind, and my immediate thought was that the canister was a much publicized container of arms, radios and other essentials for the rumoured spies, insurgents or whatever.

Both Dad and I thought we should at least see how to open the thing and find out just what its contents were. With only the reflected light from searchlights it was not apparent quite how to do this. Dad thought he might have some tools to aid our quest.

For my part, I was reluctant to do too much about it as by then I imagined that a Nazi spy cell disguised as nuns would emerge over the crest of the hill from the other side of the bridge to claim their goodies.

All our speculation was suddenly brought to an end by the arrival on the scene of a local retired naval officer and eccentric. Although he had come undefined connections with the ARP, he was brandishing a sword and shouting foul imprecations about the rumoured Nazi hordes and what he intended to do to them. In the middle of all this a local bobby appeared as if by magic and managed to calm things down. He, it seemed, was fairly well clued up about things dropped by German raiders and informed us all that the thing was a land mine and we should make ourselves scarce while he contacted his station to find out what he should do about it.

Bennett and his father made their way back to their almost win-
dowless house and joined his mother, younger sisters and brothers. Soon an ARP warden advised them to evacuate the area, which
the seven of them did:

THE RAID ONE NIGHT was intensifying and thoughts turned
toward taking refuge in our host's Anderson shelter. But there
was no way it could hold the nine of us.

It was finally decided that at least the four children should be
stowed away in the relative security the shelter offered. No
sooner was this done than the customary whoosh and ground-
shaking thump heralded the arrival of a bomb nearby. It tran-
spired that this had not exploded, so once again it was
whistle-and-warden time, and "Evacuate the premises."

Our hosts had relatives fairly close who they were sure could
accommodate them, but not the again-dispossessed seven. After
some discussion with such ARP personnel as could be found, our
family was on the road again, this time heading for an emergency reception centre for refugees at Barnes Green.

This was some two to three miles distant, it was gone midnight
and the raid was still worsening. I recall that at one stage during this
trek I put my status-symbol steel helmet on the head of my youngest
brother, who was still being trundled along in his push chair. Only
afterward I wondered how he reacted to the weight of this, but at the
time his safety seemed to be the priority as shrapnel from exploding
ack-ack shells was bouncing off the curbs. (However, he did reach
maturity without rounded shoulders or a permanent stoop.)

When we arrived at the reception centre at Barnes it was full,
and we were told to go to the Odeon cinema at the junction of
upper Richmond Road and Sheen Lane. After a two-mile trudge
back on our tracks, we arrived and were admitted to the doubt-
ful security of the cinema. Hundreds of people were milling
about in the aisles, but eventually order prevailed and we gratefully organized ourselves in some seats.

I can remember officials of various sorts made "putting you in the picture" announcements from the stage. At what I suppose was just before 6 A.M., my father left us to go to work — he was on the six-to-two shift at Watney's Brewery. The all-clear had sounded a short while before, much to the relief of the captive audience of late-night cinema goers. The film show had been quite well received, but it had been difficult to concentrate on plots punctuated by earth tremors and explosions of nearby bombs.

Our refugee status took an upward turn shortly after Dad had gone. Cups of hot steaming tea were dispensed, and pies or pasties steaming hot from the local bakery were distributed among the masses.

The feeding of the five thousand was never as good as this.

Esther Cutting made her way out of her house on Sunday morning, September 8, and watched as hundreds of people congregated at the local school preparing to evacuate to a safe area:

IT HAD BEEN ARRANGED that a fleet of buses would take them where they had to go. The people were mainly elderly or young women with their children.

The buses did not arrive, so it was arranged that the people would spend the night in the school. That night the school was heavily bombed and very few people got out alive.

The Luftwaffe returned just before Sunday lunch, but in smaller numbers, and again attacked the docks. Once again the fire engines raced to get the new fires under control. The worst fires were at the Surrey Docks. The heat was so great that paint on the fire-fighting boats on the far bank blistered. Flaming pieces of wood were thrown into the sky, and when they settled, ignited new fires. As the warehouses caught fire, so did the goods inside. One contained barrels of rum, and each exploding barrel threw burning liquor everywhere.

Nell had enough of sheltering by the rubbish bins for one day and refused to return. Instead she prepared Alf's dinner. For once Alf cancelled his Sunday lunchtime visit to the local pub and stayed on the roof of the building watching the approaching German aircraft.

After another night of heavy bombing, weary Londoners returned to work on Monday morning. There were still fires raging unchecked and many of the collapsed buildings had uncounted bodies lying in them. Volunteers could be seen, with torn clothing and covered with dust, picking and pulling at the rubble. Police stood guard at the corner of many streets, warning those attempting to enter of unexploded bombs waiting for the bomb-disposal units.

It is difficult to imagine a more dangerous job than that of the bomb-disposal crews. Major Godfrey Ovens was posted to London in 1940:

IN ONE early big raid we were called to assist in digging out some unfortunates, residents in a guest house that had been hit. The bombs were still whistling down and when one whistle seemed to be coming down on me, I dropped to the ground and cowered in the gutter alongside the guest-house rubble. Lying face down with my steel helmet on the back of my head I felt a nudge in my back. I looked up and there I saw a diminutive ARP lass who said, "What you want, luv? A nice hot cuppa?"

On another occasion I was dealing with a UXB [unexploded bomb] adjacent to a railway line and near a row of houses. The area had been evacuated pending the time the bomb was made safe. When the bomb had been exposed, all engaged personnel retired to a safe distance, while I prepared to defuse the bomb.

I was just about to descend the excavation to the bomb when I saw a movement nearby. There was a chap peering over the garden fence. I asked him why he was not away at a safe distance like everyone else. He replied, "I could see you were an officer, so I thought it can't be dangerous if there's an officer hanging around." The chap had served in the First World War.

Another time I had successfully defused a UXB in the garden of a large house, which was threatening a factory nearby. The bomb had penetrated the ground fairly deeply, so we had to make a large excavation. The excavated material was piled alongside the digging.

When the all-clear was given the house owners were allowed to return to their homes. The owner of the house from whose garden we had taken the bomb watched it being loaded.

I was about to get on my motorbike to go to the next job when he approached me and, pointing to the excavation works, said, "What about all that?"

One of my sappers [assistants], who overheard him, said, "Don't worry about that, guv. The bloke from Kew Gardens will be around to make it tidy and ask what plants you want to put in."

The night raids were not easy to stop. There was no radar in the Spitfire and Hurricane, and the pilots who were so effective against the daylight attackers found that unless the visibility was almost perfect they had little chance of seeing the enemy. It was to the ack-ack gunners that Londoners looked for protection.

Before the war it was felt that 480 heavy anti-aircraft guns positioned around the capital should do the trick. On the day the enemy arrived there were 264 guns. By the end of the first day not one of the hundreds of bombers that had attacked the docks had been shot down. In fact it was not until nine in the evening that the city's defences made any noise at all.

It was no fault of the men who had been in action throughout the day: the sound locators on which the batteries relied for accuracy proved to be ineffective. The government was racing to correct the problem; but on this day they realized that to stop a German attack by night was almost impossible.

The bombing continued on the docks for four more days and nights. Although much has been written about the bravery of the East Ender, the truth is that the first days of bombing forced many to leave their homes and look for safety out of the area. And who could blame them? The Luftwaffe attacks were relentless. No sooner had the all-clear sounded than more bombers could be heard approaching.

As the raids continued, provision for the homeless became critical as rest centres quickly became overcrowded. Adding to those who had been bombed out were those who had been forced to leave their homes because of the hundreds of unexploded bombs yet to be defused. The bomb-disposal units were vastly under-manned and their members had received only the most basic of training. Fortunately one in 10 bombs that fell on London were duds. Some were defective and others had a delayed time fuse set to explode anytime. The Royal Engineers, who had to deal with them, were extremely short of personnel. Thousands of bombs waited for the engineers to arrive. Great numbers of people made their way from their homes to the already crowded rest centres to wait until bombs parked on their streets had been moved or defused. The most famous of these bombs was one that fell on the night of September 12 and lodged itself close to the foundations of St. Paul's Cathedral.

It was finally removed by a bomb-disposal squad and driven with great haste to the Hackney Marshes where it was dumped. The resulting explosion caused a crater a hundred feet in diameter.

Surprisingly most people continued to work throughout the bombardment. The eight hours they could spend working beside friends helped them to take their minds away from what was happening outside.

The moment an air-raid alert was sounded all employers were obligated to send their workers to the basements of their buildings for shelter. Many working hours were lost because the sirens often sounded for a small raid that would have had little or no effect on the workers' safety. Because of this, Churchill brought in a scheme that called for roof spotters. Only when the alarm was given by a spotter would the workers be sent to the safety of shelters.

Looting was also a problem, as some took advantage of the shops and houses that were without their windows and doors. Children found in the bombed-out homes dangerous new playgrounds, and in between the raids gathered pieces of shrapnel as souvenirs.

Nell had found the ideal shelter. The nearby tube station. Regularly, at seven each evening, she joined hundreds of others carrying their bedding toward the deep underground stations.

The idea of spending every night in a tube station had been born a few days after the opening raids, when thousands of East Enders refused to leave the stations they had taken over as temporary shelters. Officials had planned to use the stations for the injured and to transport troops. Thousands of Londoners using them for shelter was certainly not what they'd had in mind. With the help of police and transport officials, they tried to prevent people from bedding down on the platforms but were overwhelmed by crowds who had bought tickets to travel and then simply refused to leave.

Within days more than 150,000 had found the deep tube stations quite to their liking.

Alf refused to join them. The dread of undressing in front of strangers far outweighed the danger of a bomb. He would continue to spend his evenings beside the radio with his newspapers close at hand.

Many felt the same way. In future raids it was estimated that 64 percent preferred their own beds to the shelters and took cover only when the bombs appeared to be dropping particularly close to home.

But when Marie Lewis came off night duty at her local railway station she would go straight to Bethnal Green tube station:

I WOULD BE so tired that I would lie down on the concrete platform. All around me were men, women and children sleeping. When the last tube trains came in, passengers stepped over the people lying there — rows and rows of us.

One Saturday there was almost continuous bombing for so many hours starting from the afternoon. The docks were set alight and even when darkness fell, you could read a newspaper in the street from the glow of the fires. It was like Dante's Inferno!

Sometimes the bombing was so bad that ambulance men had to use sacks to pick up the pieces of bodies. No one could ever say for sure that we would see the next day, yet we sang anyway.

My husband came home on leave and the evening he came home we tried to make up for lost time. Suddenly, without warning, there was a terrific crash and our ceiling came down on us just as we were making love! To say the earth moved for us is an understatement!

For the poor of the East End the shelter became a second home, and in these dismal surroundings a remarkable people grew strongly defiant. They would hold out against whatever Goering could dish out.

Some, like Jean Taplin, needed help to overcome their fear:

I WAS in such a state when we had the air raids, I would go to the shelter with a pot in one hand I used to be sick in.

Gordon Tothill was living in London in the area where the underground Northern line came above ground:

THIS WAS a favourite target of the Germans, so the houses on our street were a bit of a mess. They had an air-raid shelter in the park, but I wouldn't go down there. My mother threatened all kinds of things, but it was an awful place. There were just concrete benches along a wall that you were supposed to sleep on. They were so narrow I kept falling off. We tried taking these little Lilo beds, which you blew air into, but they would go flat in the night, so you were back where you started. Anyway, the bombing got pretty bad and they had a mobile ack-ack gun that used to boom! boom! right outside our house, and what with the searchlight at the end of the street, my mother finally said, "I've had enough of this. You're going into the park shelter and that's final." So off we went.

Next morning when we came back home, we saw a bomb had fallen just a few doors down. There wasn't a window left in our house and the doors were all blown in and my bed was absolutely peppered with shards of glass, long pieces sticking out of the pillow. Eventually we got a Morrison shelter. I remember having the job of putting this together because, with no dad, someone had to do it. I'd cut myself at school pretty bad and had one hand in a sling, so there I was working with my left hand lifting these huge pieces of metal to form a table shelter in the basement.

The sirens would go and we'd all climb under the table. Eventually I'd find myself staying in bed despite all the shouts from my mother.

The need for drivers, ambulance workers, wardens or firemen became desperate.

M. Fitzgerald set off to join the ARP:

I HAD A MORRIS ISIS CAR and when I reported to the council depot they said, "Can we use your car, too?" I said yes, and they put four stretchers on the top of the car. We used to do 24 hours on and 24 hours off all for three pounds a week. We used to practise first aid on each other, and that was all right at first, but when the real thing started that was a different story. One night the bombs were falling all over the East End and we were kept very busy, and just nearby was a block of flats. An air-raid alert was on, and we could see a German plane flying in the sky. We never heard any bombs drop, but a man came running into the depot with a child in his arms all bleeding. The man was shouting, "For God's sake help us! A bomb has dropped on the flats." I said to three of my mates, "Come on, let's go!" but the supervisor said, "You can't go until you fill out an incident report." I said, "There are people up there who need our help." So a couple of ARP blokes got in the car and we went to the flat.

It was about two o'clock in the morning and was very dark as I drove around the building. I was expecting to see rubble and bricks everywhere, but there were only a few bricks lying on the pavement.

We went into the flats and it was pitch dark, and we heard somebody shouting for help. We went in and there it was. A bomb! It had gone through the first floor and straight through to the ground floor, which the people were using as a shelter. The women and kids were lying around the edges of the room and the men had been in the centre playing cards. The bomb had dropped right in the middle of them. It was chaos. They were all covered in bricks and rubble and were crying and groaning. We started to dig them out. We dug one young fellow out, and as I pulled him up by the armpits half his body came away. He was dead so I dragged him outside and put him up against the wall. His eyes were wide open, looking at the sky. I went back inside and helped pull a young girl out, and she only had one leg and she kept crying and saying, "My leg hurts!" I was glad every night when my 24 hours were up and I could go down the tube for a sleep. I was called up in the army about a year later. I was glad to get in the army for a rest.

Those who joined the ARP or Fire Service, who just a few months before had heard whispers accusing them of seeking out a "cushy number," were heroes. Some had no experience, but through grit and determination flung themselves, with little regard for their own safety, into buildings in danger of falling.

Frank Tolliss and other members of his crew of the London Auxiliary Fire Service came from all walks of life:

THEY WERE mainly barrow boys [street-cart food vendors] from Camden Town and nearby Queens Crescent, but we also had actors, a cinema attendant, a building plasterer and an accountant. A pretty mixed bunch of lads, but the barrow boys were the ones to see that we were comfortable and as well fed as possible.

Despite the constant danger, life went on and new life made its appearance with the help of people like Dorothy Lowman, a nurse who got her training in midwifery in the height of wartime:

BABIES HAVE a habit of making their first appearance in the middle of the night. With the blackout it was not always easy to find the address. Some were just rooms, or one room suspended amongst the ruins of a building. Some were houses on long streets where many homes had been devastated. It was usual when one was sent to a mother who had started labour to go in advance of the midwife, to prepare and stay with the expectant mother, and to send for the midwife when the birth was imminent.

On this occasion the house was small, the windows almost on the street with a narrow pavement separating. It was a young girl living with her mother. Mum had put a mattress on the floor in the small cluttered kitchen in back. Mum was a very stout lady, wearing a pinafore that was once white, a pair of nearly black plimsolls with holes cut to give her bunions freedom.

Like all the other East Enders I'd met, they had hearts of gold.

I had to kneel on the floor to see to the mother-to-be, which, after a time, was rather back-aching work. The sirens went and almost immediately the street became full of people heading for the shelter. They all seemed to know what was happening on the kitchen floor, and as they passed they tapped on the window and shouted things like, "How yer gettin' on, mate?"

"Mate" was progressing satisfactorily to the accompaniment of bombs whizzing through the air. I was grateful when the midwife arrived in time for the actual delivery, as legally I was not qualified to do it on my own.

A lovely baby was produced, and eventually mother and baby were settled on the mattress under the table. The midwife and myself found our way home in the blackout between the bombs.

Peggy Mason (now Barwell) was living at the Elephant and Castle in London. She was 24 years old and nine months pregnant:

ON OCTOBER 17 my labour pains started. I prayed for a quiet evening. Please, God, no bombing. At 7:30 P.M. I tucked my two little girls into bed under the kitchen table (downstairs). The sirens sounded. It had started. I could hear the swish of bombs overhead.

I peeped out the blackout and the sky was alight with gunfire. The bombs were falling nearer. I paced the floor. The windows shook. Doors banged. My children were scared. The midwife arrived. She had cycled three miles through the air raid to get to me.

My baby, a girl, was born at 10 P.M. with the bombs falling all around us.

Joan Room started her nursing career at London's Fulham Hospital in 1940. She'd gone on a shopping expedition with a couple of colleagues:

ON OUR WAY BACK we noticed a big formation of planes very high in the sky. It was a very lovely clear September afternoon, we were happy and the sight didn't cause us any disturbance. We went to tea in the dining room in the nurses' home and later went to our rooms.

As dusk and then darkness fell, we prepared to go to our sleeping quarters, which were bunks in the tunnel leading from the main hospital to the nurses' home on the other side. We pulled our curtains — lights off, of course — and it seemed as if the whole of London was on fire.

The bombing continued on through Sunday, and on Monday morning a bomb fell on Fulham Hospital. The noise was deafening — dust and dirt were in the air — the smell of the explosion is something I shall never forget.

We dressed in our usual uniforms and went on duty although it was hours earlier than our normal 7:30 A.M. start. We were directed to prepare patients for immediate evacuation.

The water mains had burst as a result of the bombing, so we were without water supply. I was given about one-third of a cup of water, and with the bib of my apron filled with cotton wool I was sent to swab clean the nose and mouth of each patient. (Washing was out of the question.) It still amazes me that there was no panic or sign of fear. We juniors acted as though everything was normal.

The only drinks available were undiluted fruit juices for staff and patients alike. The patients were soon on their way to other hospitals by bus, car and ambulance, and we nurses were sent to search the rubble for anything we might find, i.e., false teeth, specs, photos and the like.

As I went about my business, a photographer handed me a cat and asked me to stand for a photograph. I was too shy and gave the cat to another nurse close by. The next day the centre page of *The Daily Mail* showed two pictures. One of the bombed hospital with black headlines "Another Hospital Bombed by the Huns" and "Brave Nurses Rescue Hospital Cat."

Leslie Jerman figured Hitler did one good thing by bombing London:

> HE DROVE the bed bugs out of our house — they had no one there to feed on!

Photo reconnaissance had shown that the invasion ports along the French coast were filling up with Nazi shipping, and four captured German spies claimed that Hitler's preparations for an invasion by sea were now complete. Everyone agreed that Hitler needed to invade before the winter, only a month or so away.

Britain's code word for an imminent invasion was "Cromwell," and during the attack on London this was the word sent around the country. Unfortunately many could not remember whether "Cromwell" meant that one should merely be on guard for an invasion or that German troops had actually landed. In one location, thinking the latter, British troops began blowing up bridges. In another the local Home Guard began to ring church bells, signalling that the invasion had begun. In the small villages strangers with foreign accents were looked on with suspicion, and on the coast all eyes were turned to the sea.

Although buoyed by the exaggerated claims of the Luftwaffe, Hitler continued to have serious doubts about an invasion. Reports from the Nazi propagandist Joseph Goebbels about the chaos, terror and defeat in London had been good news, but other intelligence sources seemed to suggest that Londoners were settling down and accepting the raids as routine. Admiral Raeder, who had never been completely sold on the idea of an invasion, felt that not only were the risks too great, but any success in resisting such a landing would give the British a powerful boost — at a time when the Luftwaffe was making strides to undermine their confidence.

Moreover, the British *were* expecting a landing and would be prepared. Raeder suggested that an invasion should be postponed for now, and Hitler agreed. Two days later he announced that Operation Sea Lion would be postponed indefinitely.

Hitler was happier to occupy himself with thoughts of swallowing a much bigger fish. Russia. In the meantime Goering could continue to amuse himself by crushing Britain from the sky.

This proved a blessing for Churchill. He had still to replace the mountains of equipment left at Dunkirk, and although the people were ready psychologically for the invasion, physically they were not equipped.

Edward Skinner, a London policeman, was standing in Trafalgar Square on Sunday, September 8:

IT WAS ABOUT 11 A.M. The siren had sounded when overhead I saw a German plane, a Dornier, being chased by two Hurricanes. One of them flew under the Dornier. The tail unit of the German plane was shot away and fell outside a Pimlico pub. Two of the crew parachuted out and landed on the Oval cricket ground in Kennington. The main section crashed on the roof of Walkers jewellers, then situated in the forecourt of Victoria Station. One Hurricane with Pilot Officer Holmes went out of control and he bailed out and landed on a Chelsea roof.

According to the news reports, the Germans were chased around the Oval ground by local housewives with brooms.

The bomb load had already been dropped. One landed in the grounds of Buckingham Palace.

Although Edward Skinner reports that both RAF planes were Hurricanes, one was in fact a Spitfire being flown by Squadron Leader Skeets Ogilvie:

I HAD made an attack with my squadron and flown through what looked like the whole German air force — a mass of

German aircraft — and was on my way round to make another attack. I was sort of on my own and as I pulled up to get in position I saw this one German guy, a Dornier 17. He must have been in trouble, lagging along behind the others. So I attacked him from the side. A gunner returned the fire, then it stopped. I went round for a second attack and the crew started bailing out. One of them came out of the aircraft and went just over the top of my head.... I thought he was going to go right into the prop...scared the hell out of me.

Then when the crew bailed out, the aircraft started twisting. It was an amazing sight — it just broke apart in the air. The tail floated away and the wings just snapped off.... The main part was the part, I suppose, that landed on Victoria Station.

A week later the Air Ministry received a letter from Queen Wilhelmina of The Netherlands, who was living in London during the war and had been watching the action. She wrote to congratulate Ogilvie's group, the 109 Fighter Squadron.

The news that a bomb had actually fallen in the grounds of Buckingham Palace was a reminder that the family living in that large house was the same as any other — well, almost.

The Queen later said that she was glad she had been bombed: "It makes me feel we can look the East End in the face."

But Harold Nicholson describes the East Enders as hardly forgiving:

EVERYBODY is worried about the feeling in the East End, where there is much bitterness. It is said that even the King and Queen were booed the other day when they visited the destroyed areas. Clem says that if only the Germans had the sense not to bomb west of London Bridge there might be a revolution in this country. As it is, they have smashed Bond Street and Park Lane, and so readjusted the balance.

Because the bombing appeared confined to poorer areas, bad feelings had been growing steadily. Constantly on the look-out for a place to hide, the East Enders were not happy to hear about luxury deep shelters beneath the posh hotels and expensive stores. Moreover, the wealthy appeared to be living as high as they had during peacetime. Certainly the clubs were doing a roaring business, and those fortunate enough to be members could forget the troubles of war. To make matters worse, it was not uncommon to see wealthy groups making their way home from the West End theatres via the subway shelters, amusing themselves by observing how the other half lived.

In the months to come, however, they would have little time for such "tours." The bombing raids of the Luftwaffe expanded to cover a much wider area. For the next 76 nights, with the exception of November 2 when the weather was too bad for flying, London, Europe's largest city, would receive the full fury of the German air force.

9

LIFE UNDERGROUND

ON SEPTEMBER 15 Nell and her two daughters bundled up their things and left the tube for home. It was another hot summer day, and as Nell made her way up the stairs of the building she felt good. Her family had suffered no injuries or deaths, and despite the conditions were remarkably fit. She had heard that there had been a dramatic rise in tuberculosis among people living in shelters. She was glad she had agreed to evacuate her son to the country.

She opened the door and found Alf with breakfast and the Sunday newspapers. Most of the news concerned the war, from information on treating injured pets and livestock to the number of soccer games forced to cancel. Advertisements told Londoners who had the money that they could get away from it all: "Nice

Quiet Hotel away from the Bombing," or "Safe and Sunny with Peaceful Nights." Space devoted to the weather described conditions off Dover and what this might mean to an invader.

There was no suggestion that September 15 would be a day like no other and go down in the pages of British history as "The Battle of Britain Day." It was the day that marked the turning point in the battle. Above London alone on that day 350 planes, manned by every pilot Britain had, were engaged in combat.

After the first week of heavy bombing, the people in those areas most under attack began to get into a routine. Straight after supper they prepared their bedding and headed for the shelters. Those forced to use the major shelters found themselves faced with the problem of overcrowding. The Tilbury shelter, in the East End, was one of the worst. This massive goods yard, under a railway station in Stepney, suddenly found itself home to 15,000 people a night, jammed in head to toe and attempting to sleep on the cold concrete floors, along with the rats and excrement. Yet despite the conditions, every afternoon saw huge line-ups of people waiting to get into this dungeon.

When the doors finally opened there was a mad scramble for the better spots, which were the ones farthest from the stench of the open buckets used as toilets.

It was the same in the tube stations. People were packing the platforms and, when these were full, trying to find places to sleep on the stairs. Once the power was turned off at 10:30 P.M. and the trains stopped running, many climbed down onto the rails and vanished into the tunnels to find spots to stretch out. There was no sanitation or washing facilities on the platforms, and people could be seen walking down the tunnels to find a private place to relieve themselves.

Seven-year-old Esme Temple was taking the tube train to visit her sister's future in-laws:

I CRIED when I saw all the people sleeping on the underground platforms in the centre of London. There must have been people there in the mornings, as well as afternoons, but I was left with a shocked sad feeling. Many of the platforms were not wide, and a white line was drawn behind which people who had to sleep there stayed. Men who did night work and slept during the day had to curl up, and if their toes and legs were stretched over the line the guard would come over with a long pole and shove the sleeping men's legs back over the white line.

Yet a strange sense of camaraderie was born among those attempting to make the most of living below the ground. One man, Micky Davies, who was hunched of back and only four feet tall, became a legend.

He made his home in a Stepney shelter that housed 10,000 in the most appalling conditions. An optician by trade, he had lost his tiny shop in an earlier raid. He was a natural organizer, and soon brought order to the chaos. He divided the shelter into three groups — families, single men and single women.

Eventually all the shelters made similar groupings, and formed committees to push the government into action. Toilet facilities were installed and bunks were built in the shelters and tubes, which improved living conditions greatly. The double-tier bunks made it possible for parents to bed down their children and sit quietly by as they went to sleep.

Nell had a regular spot in the Borough tube station close to London Bridge, which was just a five-minute walk from her home. The last train of the day had pushed clean air through the platform, and most of the families were settling down to sleep. She set her alarm clock for 4 A.M. and placed it alongside her tin helmet, close to her head.

Elizabeth Hodgkiss was six years old at the beginning of the war and most of her friends had been evacuated. The Auxiliary Fire Service took over her school, leaving just one classroom:

THERE WERE about six or seven of us with one teacher. When an air raid sounded we all moved to sit cross-legged under the big table in the hall, and lessons continued as normal.

Those of us who were left in London became quite used to the routine of the early evening. For a while my family sheltered in our own Anderson shelter, but then we found, like everyone, that going down the tube was preferable. The children were in siren suits, and mothers carried whatever they thought they might need — food, blankets, comics. There was no rush, no panic, just a stream of people making for the shelter where we children would find our friends and have a noisy game before settling down for the night. The trains still ran, of course, and I remember we had to sleep on the platforms and there was a painted white line beyond which we were not allowed to lie. The stations still had to cope with passengers.

After the last train, of course, it got much better — and if we continued to go down the tube regularly (and were lucky) we could even be allocated a steel bunk. I did eventually get to sleep on one, but it wasn't very comfortable.

Tickets were issued to regulars in the shelters to reserve a particular bunk. Evening classes in all sorts of skills were begun and it was not uncommon to find one group learning dressmaking and another nearby rehearsing a play. With so many strangers thrown together, it was no surprise to find that there was no lack of talent ready to help pass the hours.

Flora Wood lived in Tottenham, London:

NEAR US there was and still is a big park, half of which in those days was allotments for shelters. It was decided by the council to do away with these and construct one huge shelter, as we were such a thickly populated area.

On the day the shelter was opened, I think by the mayor, it was with a band and everybody rejoicing. It was either the day or night afterward that the shelter got a direct hit. They didn't even bother to dig the people in it out, there were so many. We had a letter from the council asking us to watch for empty houses and report if we hadn't seen the usual people around. This was the only way they knew who was down there.

Raf pilots were the heroes of the day. Johnny Johnson tells what it felt like:

I WAS in London during the blitz. I had been spending the night in London and I had to get back to my unit, so in the early hours of the morning I set out for the underground. I was obliged to walk down a rather long tube station where everybody was just getting up.

Now, I was a sergeant pilot and had just got my wings, but I had never flown an actual operational aircraft.

I was 18 years old. All these people saw this laddie in blue with a pair of wings on and they all cheered. I had to walk down this platform with them all cheering, and you can just imagine the effect that this had on a young man of 18 to be cheered like this, like a hero, by all these people who were suffering all sorts of things. It was pretty heady stuff.

Florence Pond (now Morgan) was 22 when the blitz started. She was living in the East End of London:

THAT FIRST NIGHT we just sat in our Anderson shelter — so isolated. We couldn't hear any ground guns challenging them, although our fighters must have been up there the way they were in the afternoon, but as Jerry came in, wave after wave, it seemed all we could do was wait, hope and pray.

As the blitz developed into a routine, we often used to hear our anti-aircraft guns, and this was a great consolation — even if, as we have since learned in recent years from TV accounts by ground gunners at the time, "We hadn't a hope in hell of hitting the planes, but it boosted people's morale just hearing the guns." Believe me, it did!

My mother took it badly, so I arranged for her to be evacuated to some friends' at Datchet. My sister went with her and I stayed behind with my father.

Night after night in the Anderson shelter, with virtually no sleep and having to cope with work each day, was beginning to take its toll, so Dad and I decided we would go to the nearest tube station each night — at least there you had a chance of getting some rest.

Our nearest tube was Bethnal Green — an unfinished station, as work had been halted on it owing to the war. People not only slept on the platform, but on the railway tracks, as well. Our regular place was right alongside the railway track into one part of the tunnel.

Our house was now damaged so much it was uninhabitable (mainly because of a bomb that fell only a few houses away in our terraced street). Dad and I accepted living that meant going from work to a place for eats and the tube for sleep. We used to keep our bundle of bedclothes for the tube at work. How we ever kept clean during the period amazes me.

At the time I was only engaged to my husband, who was then in the RAF. His family sheltered all night in a local communal warehouse on the Isle of Dogs, which was on the dock's edge and had been reinforced for the bombing and fitted with bunks. When he was home on leave my father and I would also go to this shelter so we could all be together, but I never felt safe there.

I am sorry to say that my fears were confirmed when this shelter eventually took a direct hit — many people were killed or injured. Immediately I heard about it, I telephoned my fiancé for details. All his family, mother, father, two sisters and brother had been injured, and a sister of 19 was reported missing. Then we learned that she had actually been brought out on the night it happened. Dead.

The funeral of his sister, so young, I shall never forget. They draped a Union Jack over her coffin and she was buried in a communal grave, which must have been the only way then of coping with all the casualties everywhere at the time. But the most impressive sight was the journey to the cemetery. She had worked for a large food company, and the employees, all there in their white overalls and hats, lined part of the route on each side of the road whilst the funeral passed.

Audrey Bown's father had a greengrocery in southwest London. She was 13 and remembers going to a shelter every night under the premises of a United Dairies shop:

WE WENT ARMED with rugs, and my mother and I wore thick navy serge trousers — the first time either of us had ever worn such garments. There we would sit upright on hard benches until the all-clear next morning (there were too many people crammed in to lie down).

As one can imagine, the air became very, very foul by the end of the night, and one day my parents decided we would spend the next night in an area under the stairs at our home. It was a big four-storey house with a substantial staircase, and the night of Friday the 13th of September 1940 found us in three deck-chairs, together with three members of the Baker family from up the road, whom we had invited to share our shelter.

There was an anti-aircraft placement on Clapham Common and the noise from that, as well as from bombs exploding in the vicinity, was terrific. Sometime during that night the bomb fell that was to change my life forever. I believe it fell on the nearby cosmetic factory, but I can only recall everything falling down around us. Miraculously the staircase held, but the only way to the street was through the shop, which was in ruins with piles of

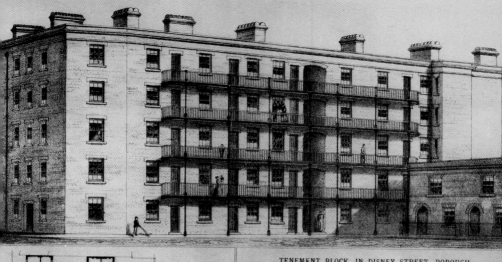

TENEMENT BLOCK, IN DISNEY STREET, BOROUGH,

FOR THE

Workmen's Dwellings Improvement Company, Limited

OFFICES: 121, PALL MALL, LONDON, S.W.

FRANK E. THICKE, ARCHITECT, 5, GREAT QUEEN STREET, WESTMINSTER.

e: St George's
ings in London's
End, the home of
and Alf Wicks and
family.

: Gas-mask cases
sold in the street,
efore the outbreak
r.

um Picture Library)

Above: Many buildings were reduced to uninhabitable shells, recognizable only by the wallpaper and the few hangings left on the interior walls.
(Topham Picture Library)

Left: An injured woman is helped to a reception centre after her home has been bombed in a raid on Liverpool, May 1941.
(The Trustees of the Imperial War Museum, London)

Above: Local inhabitants inspect bomb damage in Gravesend, Kent, 1940. *(Topham Picture Library)*

Right: Sacred relics: a priest surveys the damage at Lamorbey Church in Sidcup, Kent, 1940. *(Topham Picture Library)*

London Underground stations became places of both refuge and entertainment: above, people sleeping on the platform at Piccadilly, and below, a concert given by the ENSA (Entertainments National Services Association) at Aldwych.
(Above: Topham Picture Library; Below: The Hulton–Deutsch Collection)

Above: Many homes had their own air-raid shelters, sometimes in unexpected places—like this one, concealed among the cabbages at the bottom of the garden.
(Topham Picture Library)

Right: A family in London's East End is taken in by neighbours after their home—visible across the road—has been bombed.
(The Trustees of the Imperial War Museum, London)

Right: Many shelters, like this one, were built and shared by several neighbouring families, with an entrance from each garden.
(Topham Picture Library)

Below: A mother demonstrates the newly invented gas-proof pram, December 1938. Made of wood, it incorporated a triplex glass window, an air-valve, a filter and a large bulb at the rear to pump out the air.
(Topham Picture Library)

Five hospitals were among the buildings hit during London's
heaviest raid of 1941. Here, nurses clear up debris in the grounds
and restore one of the damaged wards to order.
(Above and below: Topham Picture Library)

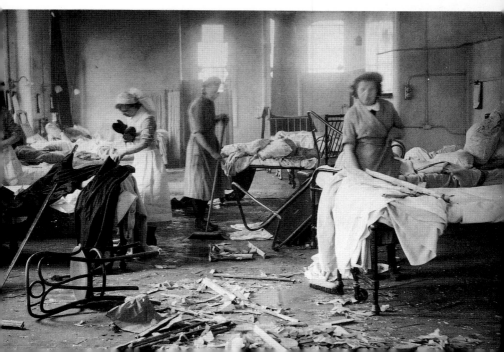

Left: Salvaging treasured possessions from a bombed house, October 1940.
(The Trustees of the Imperial War Museum, London)

Below: Shelters were sometimes decorated for special occasions, such as this concert in Westminster
(Topham Picture Library)

broken glass everywhere. I remember my father pulling me through the glass, pieces of which were still falling around us, and into the street.

There, it was absolute mayhem. Ack-ack guns going at full strength, still more bombs exploding and the sky lit up with piercing searchlights. To add to the nightmare, horses were running amok from some nearby stables, but somehow we succeeded in reaching the trapdoor to the shelter under the United Dairies, and Father hammered on it for us to be let in.

Eventually someone lifted the trapdoor and my mother promptly fell down the perpendicular flight of steps to the shelter below. Subsequently we found she had fractures to her hands, but it was amazing she had no more serious injuries (she was, however, to become an invalid for the rest of her life). I was told that I passed out in the shelter, but can only recall the horrible taste of some liquid in a beery glass someone was forcing me to drink.

I remember the great joy I felt a few days later when Dad had managed to rescue my cat. The cat had been trapped, unable to move, for several days, but was uninjured. Instead of being a tabby, however, it was white with bomb blast.

Margaret Hoyle was working in a London shop. Since the bombing made it impossible for her to get home during the evening raids, arrangements were made in the shop basement:

IT WAS FITTED OUT with two sections — male and female. There was a kitchen and a rota amongst the girls for cooking breakfast.

In the evening a crowd of us would link arms and go out into the blackout to Marble Arch for our meal at Lyons Corner House. The sirens always went at 6:30 P.M. and several times on our return we had to lie flat on the pavement up against the shops during a raid. We were always thankful to get back to our "dormitory," with its rows of hospital beds.

It was all great fun until the night of intense bombing and incendiaries on Oxford Street, and the John Lewis department store was ablaze from end to end.

When we emerged in the early morning to view the extensive damage the store was still burning. Our back entrance went out into Harley Street, and hanging across the corner of a building was a parachute with a land mine dangling over the edge.

After that I decided to join the Auxiliary Territorial Service (ATS) and became a radar operator on heavy ack-ack gun sites, so felt I was doing my bit to fight back.

A. Gabe was a member of the Ambulance Service. He'd just been called to a "deep shelter" in south London:

THE ENTRANCE was in the borough High Street and was sandbagged, fairly wide, and once inside, we found a gradual incline to a flight of wooden planking stairs. I think my mate and I counted 120. Dim electric lighting, terrible stench of dank, cold air and quite a few hundred people, men, women, children, babies in arms, but the air was so heavy that when we carried our patient on the stretcher or a chair back to the top, we were covered in perspiration and really gasping for air.

They used to call it the deep shelter, and it really was!

Joyce Mason lived in southeast London in a downstairs flat. She and her family stayed in the kitchen, diving under the table, when they heard a string of bombs:

I WELL REMEMBER one evening putting the saucepan on the stove full of milk and then when we emerged finding it full of soot. When it was bedtime, my mother, myself, my husband (when home) and the lady who lived upstairs used to come down. The elderly gentleman she looked after was extremely deaf, so he wouldn't take any notice of the raids.

We put a wardrobe at a slant in a corner and put a bucket behind it to make a little privacy for the toilet.

As September rolled into October, the Luftwaffe did not confine itself to London. Random bombings took place in cities all over the country, and shelters became a way of life for everyone.

Patricia Sample (now Kelly) arrived home in Manchester from evacuation. She visited a friend of her father's, who had a pub in the borough of Deansgate:

THE SIRENS went about 7:30 P.M. We didn't take much notice at first and then the bombing became really heavy. We all went down to the underground canal that runs beneath Deansgate. It was full of beds as far as I could see. The men, including my father, were asked to volunteer putting out fires from incendiary bombs. My mother and I thought we would never see him again. The noise and the thuds were terrifying. Women were fainting. The Red Cross was working nonstop and we were told that the whole of Deansgate above us was on fire and Victoria Station had gone. Most of the exits were blocked and people were trying not to panic, but many were suffering from claustrophobia and rushing from exit to exit only to find them blocked by fallen buildings.

Eventually, to my joy, we caught sight of my father. He came down the original exit, which was still unblocked. He was exhausted after four hours of firefighting. I remember my mother saying that they were trying to extinguish incendiary bombs on the flat roofs of buildings but were greatly hampered by guard dogs on many of the properties.

We surfaced to the most devastating sight I have ever seen. We were worried about my grandma, and we eventually found our car — not a window left and covered in white ash with a half-burned-out incendiary bomb on the roof. We got in and it actually started, and we drove to All Saints. The beautiful church had gone, but thank heavens we found our gran crying outside the shop. My gran was so happy to see that we were all alive.

Jane Fabb was just four years old and living in Kent when the war started:

IN THE WEEKS prior to the outbreak of war, our next-door-but-one neighbours, Mr. and Mrs. Turner, had dug an air-raid shelter in their garden. My mother told me that everyone laughed at them — until the air raids started. The Turners generously welcomed neighbours into their shelter. It was standing room only, and my mother said that after a few nights, she couldn't cope anymore. She went back to her bed, despite the raids.

We five children from our terrace (including the Turners' two) always had bunks to sleep on in the shelter. I can remember Mrs. Turner bringing us bowls of dry cornflakes in the morning — I suppose there was no milk or sugar.

I had a Donald Duck gas mask, as did Maureen next door, but I soon grew out of it and had to have an ordinary black one, which wasn't so nice. Baby Barbara next door was put bodily into hers. A mobile gas-mask-testing unit came to the park and we went in with our gas masks on to see if they worked. They did.

There was an ARP post in the park — a little stone building, great to bounce balls against. I learned later that much hanky-panky went on there at night — well, I suppose grown-ups had to liven life up somehow.

One day my mother had queued for hours to buy a piece of liver for dinner. As she was cooking it on a summer evening with the kitchen door open to the garden, waves of German bombers came over. She later said, "I thought, my liver or my life?" She chose the liver. She sent me and Dad to the neighbours' shelter and followed later with the liver plus bits of ceiling plaster that had fallen into it when the bombs fell.

Later on the family next door to us shored up a room in their house, which was supposed to make it safe. The mother and daughter soon evacuated from London, leaving just Mr. Mayston. Mum, Dad and I used to sleep in there, in the shored-up room with Mr. Mayston. I had the indignity of sleeping in a cot as there wasn't room for my bed. My father was the chief fire watcher for our road (he was too old for the Second World War, having served in the First), so was out most nights.

It always amuses me that my mother and Mr. Mayston "slept together" unchaperoned (except by me, of course) and always addressed each other as "Mr. Mayston" and "Mrs. Webber."

I was never afraid of bombs, as my mother did a great job of showing me no fear. However, I was terrified of guns, even our own anti-aircraft ones. There was a gap between the houses opposite ours, and one day, Mum was on the phone and I was playing in our front room when a German plane dived through the gap, machine-gunning. We could see the pilot's face. Mum dropped the phone, grabbed me and threw me into the cupboard under the stairs. I could hear the bullets rattling down the roof. That frightened me. We were also machine-gunned one day as we were shopping — Mum pulled me into Sainsbury's where I was pushed under the marble counter.

Later in the war a friend's daughter, Felicity, came to stay with us. By now we had a Morrison shelter. My grandmother also lived with us much of the time, and the five of us — Mum, Dad, Grandmother, Felicity and I — had to lie "sideways on" in order to get in, so we couldn't put the fourth "cadre" side to the shelter. In later years I realized that the adults' feet must have stuck out, and I asked my mother how they managed. "When we heard a bang, we pulled our legs up," she said.

Felicity and I always thought that the knobs on the side of the shelter (which were to fix the mesh side on) were custom made for hanging up Christmas stockings, and I wondered where we would hang them when the war was over.

Whenever we blew out birthday candles or stirred the Christmas pudding (made from I know not what in those days of food shortage) the wish was always for peace. We had no idea what that was in practice, but it was evidently highly desirable.

During periods without air raids we had to sleep upstairs in beds, and this wasn't so much fun, especially as Felicity and I were in different rooms. So as we said good-night we added, "Hope there's an air raid," and my mother used to wince.

Ronald Showell was a River Thames waterman-and-lighterman licenced apprentice:

WE HAD an Anderson shelter in the backyard, and my brother, who was on leave from the RAF, dug a hole about two feet deep and set it in. (If the blitz had started a year earlier we would have had at least a foot of water in it most of the time, but the council sent round some men who concreted the holes.) Ours needed a chimney as our father would smoke. It was bloody awful.

I was in the scullery having a wash when the bombs fell. My father called out, "Are you all right?" I replied that I was, then slipped on my coat and went into the street.

I realized that two bombs had fallen. I called out, "Anybody hurt?" I heard a voice saying, "I can't get out!" The lady was in the loo. That and the scullery was all that was left of the lady's house. Once I and a neighbour had cleared away some bricks, she came out. "Thank you, young man," she said. "That was a bit close for words."

Jean Emmins had an Anderson shelter in her garden in London that six used — her family of four and two lodgers:

THE BOTTOM HALF of the shelter was under the ground, the rounded roof covered us, and at ground level there was a dirt ledge.

Father used to place boards across from ledge to ledge and the first ones down there lay on the ground and the remaining boards were then put into place once they were inside. The late-comers then lay down on a mattress and sat comfortably playing cards by candlelight before settling in for the night.

Even now the thought of me lying there completely enclosed in a three-berth coffin with a foot of headroom still gives me cold shudders!

Vicky Tunbridge may have loved to sing, but it did nothing for the state of her mother's nerves:

AS PEOPLE got used to the raids they became less inclined to use the shelter — all except my mother. She was always off like a shot as soon as that siren sounded. In fact once when I was singing away in the bath she suddenly dashed out, off to her place in the shelter.

So much for my rendition of "Down in the Valley." She thought the part where I sang "Valley so low-ow-ow" was the siren starting up. I was trying to sound like the Andrews Sisters.

John Copley remembers a remarkable woman named Miss Loring:

SHE WAS ELDERLY and unmistakably a lady in every way — the spinster daughter of a clergyman who had devoted her whole life to assisting the needy in the Bow of the 1930s.

One wild night, her house, together with everything she owned in the world, vanished utterly. My mother met her later that day. She was, as always, immaculate and apparently quite unconcerned.

"Oh, those were nothing, my dear," she said. "They're just material things. The only thing I'll miss is my little dog." Her dog still lay somewhere in the rubble.

Every night she'd conduct impromptu prayer meetings in the makeshift shelters — mere earthen-walled trenches with roofs.

She did so that night, too. After the usual prayers she startled the congregation by adding, "And now, let us pray for the Germans; that they may soon see the error of their ways before disaster overtakes them."

There were mutterings and cold stares. Many of those present had become destitute and homeless the previous night, too. Prayers for the Germans were not uppermost in their minds. Probably no other person in all of Bow could have persuaded at least some of them to remain on their knees and pray for the enemy, but somehow she did.

They don't make 'em like Miss Loring anymore; come to think of it, they didn't make too many like her even then.

Margaret Spencer was 18 and worked for Lloyds of London:

AT THE START of the blitz all Lloyds staff were instructed to go down into its deep and vast underground shelter at each alert. This refuge was a city within a city. Once in, we were sealed off completely, the object being that life could be sustained for several days, if necessary, should the building collapse. It was a very eerie sensation to be so far down into the ground, and I would have preferred to take my chances aloft. However, this exercise of going down was too time-wasting as the number of air raids increased daily. We continued thereafter working on all floors with our fingers crossed!

Lloyds was one of the few buildings that remained intact throughout the blitz.

Even if a family was lucky enough to have an Anderson shelter delivered, finding a place to put the thing was often a problem. Daisy Howell's father decided to make use of a small piece of ground at the rear of their house that backed onto Bow Road underground:

MY FATHER DUG a very deep tunnel between two old oak trees so that the top of the shelter was level with the ground. This is what really saved our lives — my mother, my father and myself.

The bombers used to follow the blue flashes of the underground trains from up the line until they disappeared into Bow Road station. We always heard the bombs whistling down as soon as the trains disappeared into the tunnel.

A bomb dropped just the other side of the railway from us, and when we came out of the shelter in the morning there were all kinds of things hanging in the trees. Clothes, sheets, bedding, eiderdowns, and in our garden someone's wardrobe, handbags, coats, stage costumes. All the things belonging to the houses that had been hit came over the railway lines with the blast and landed in our garden. My father went over to Bow Road police station, which was opposite, and they came down the street to help gather things up, which were then taken to the police station in case the people who they belonged to were all right and could collect them.

Jo Walters had arranged to go into an Anderson shelter with a friend a few doors away. Her mother-in-law, "a stout large woman," would go into the Walters' own shelter:

ONE TIME, as we heard the bang of bombs and saw lights from Molotov cocktails falling in our street, there was the funniest thing to see. We had a wire-haired terrier called Peggy, and my ma-in-law was stuck in the entrance to the shelter — with the dog under her arm barking away and her alarm clock in her other hand madly ringing.

Violet Shilling was 12 and her sister 14 when the blitz began:

MY MOTHER was expecting a baby, so my father had made a separate shelter for her and my two younger brothers in a chalk pit at the bottom of our garden. So each night we would all go to our own shelters.

When my sister and I woke up one morning we were informed that my mother had gone into hospital in the night to have her baby.

I went with my sister to tell my dad, and he came back to our house, leaving my two brothers in the shelter. The air raids in those days would start as soon as it got dark, and the all-clear would sound as soon as it got light.

We went indoors and not long afterward I heard an airplane, so I said to my dad, "Here comes a Jerry." With that he went out to the garden to find my sister. The next thing I remember was the windows rattling and I had debris all over me. I couldn't move and I could hear people trying to get me out. I was calling out, "Help! Help! I'm here. Here's my arm. Can you see it?"

I was rescued and taken to the local hospital where I received treatment for shock and concussion. I was kept in hospital about a week and kept wondering why no one came to see me, especially my dad. Then at the end of the week my dad's sister came to see me. She was all in black.

She told me that my dad and my sister had been killed.

My mum had a daughter the same day.

Doreen Barnley (now Woollard) lived in St. John's Wood, London. She had run home through the falling shrapnel:

I HAD WORKED that day until late afternoon. I was 14 years old. My 16-year-old brother had gone to the pictures "around the corner." Three families shared the house. Relations of ours, an aunt and her niece at the top. (They were already in the Anderson shelter in the garden.) The Anderson was damp and small, so we left it to them to use. The family of four in the middle flat used to join us in our basement.

My brother came home early as he could hear the racket outside the cinema, and the family of four (the Everetts) joined us in the basement.

When we heard the stick of bombs fall we all dived under a large strong table, which had been ideal for a large family to eat at and now just the job to get under for some safety.

We got well and truly blasted. Houses in the back (one where we used to live) got a direct hit, as did houses at the side of us. I was clutching my dog and facing the fireplace, which was only used part of the day. So I got the full force of soot over myself and dog.

My father herded all us women out to the Anderson shelter where we squeezed in. I had to stand (I was five foot 10) all night, still holding my little dog, who usually fought my aunt's dog. They behaved well that night — aware of the crisis, no doubt.

I cursed the Jerrys and wished one would land in my garden so that I could make him a nice cup of tea laced with cyanide.

Kathleen Heavens had an early-warning system:

IF A BOMB was dropping nearby, our parrot used to turn upside down on her perch yelling, "Ohh!" When we saw her do that we all used to dive for cover under the big double bed.

Despite being robbed of sleep by Hitler's nocturnal bombers, London continued to make the best of things. Some, like Mary Offord, did the best they could without steel helmets:

NIGHT AFTER NIGHT we would head for the Anderson shelter. We all carried a pillow which we placed over our heads every time a bomb dropped.

Word came that Rosco Street, the home of Grannie Wicks, had been hit badly. She was fine, but it had been a close call. All the

street was alight, and great big pieces were falling off the buildings.
A bomb had hit the water main and the whole street was flooded.
People were up to their ankles in water.

Her grandson went to different street shelters and in each one
asked if anyone had seen Grannie Wicks. They all knew her, as she
had been a midwife and brought most of them into the world. She
was eventually found in a deserted shelter, all scrunched up, lying
there in the corner, a little shrivelled-up old lady — but very much
alive. She took one look at her grandson and said, "You go back
'ome. I've never done anything wrong in me life and the good Lord
won't let me blow up."

Some were caught outside when the sirens sounded their warnings. Brenda Dewar was three and had been shopping with her
mother. They had just got off a single-decker bus and were on
their way home:

THERE WAS the most awful whistling sound. Mum said in a
voice of panic. "I didn't hear the siren!"

She pushed me under a clump of bushes at the grassy front
of a crescent-shaped row of maisonettes. I saw the iced buns
bought for teatime roll on the grass as Mum dropped on top of
me to protect me from the blast of the bomb. I remember an
almighty BOOM! The ground shook under me and it felt like the
sky had fallen. Mum lay so still. Then our rent collector came
from the maisonettes in the crescent and took us to a big cupboard under the stairs. There he and his wife sat Mum in a
chair and wrapped Mum's head in a huge white tablecloth. It
didn't stay white for long as the scarlet blood soon showed
through.

It seems the bomb fell in our back garden and the explosion
wrecked our maisonette and blasted tiles from the roof of the
church opposite. One of these tiles had hit Mum on the back of
the head as she lay protecting me.

In King Edward's Hospital, where they took Mum, the corridors were full of people waiting for those who had been injured, or waiting to be cleaned and patched up. So many people needed attention that screens had been put up in the corridors for makeshift dressing rooms.

Having only grazed my knee, I was my usual Nosy Parker self. My 14-year-old sister and Dad were forever dragging me back to where they were waiting news of Mum.

Dad took me to Aunt Ethel in Perivale to sleep. Something woke me in the night, and when I opened my eyes there was a faint glow in the room from the open door. I saw Dad silhouetted in the glow, and as he leaned heavily against the door he said to me, "Mummy is an angel now. I've just heard God calling her up to heaven."

Mum died on January 14, 1941.

As the mists of autumn drew in and the days got shorter, families headed for the shelters earlier each evening. The throbbing sounds of bombers overhead began to tick away a longer night.

Singsongs and other forms of entertainment were now provided in many of the shelters, and places of entertainment that had been closed during the early days of the war were now back to their regular opening times.

October 15, as on every night since the beginning of the September raids, the sirens wailed their warning. Those living in the vicinity of the Balham tube station in London gathered their bedding and headed for the deep shelter. At 8 P.M. a screaming high explosive made a direct hit on the road above the station. The ground shook and then began to sink, and a huge crater formed above one end of the platform. A mountain of earth and water poured down, blocking the passage that led to the exit. Men, women and children fought to get out of the rapidly flooding cavern.

Sixty-four died that night in the Balham tube. Never again would those making their nightly home in the underground stations feel completely safe.

The bombers that night left further devastation throughout the city — 400 killed and almost 900 seriously injured.

The three brass balls that hung outside George's pawnshop were still intact. The shop, which was at the top of the alley where Nell lived and had played a vital role in the lives of almost everyone in the area, had received a direct hit in the night.

George was picking through the ruins, trying to salvage what he could. A week earlier Nell had pawned Alf's overcoat. Now she joined George in the middle of the mess demanding to know what he was going to do about her husband's coat. "He was not happy," said Nell years later, "but eventually he got fed up wiv me moaning and handed over a coat. It was better than the one I put in, so I was happy."

Hitler may have cancelled his plans for a full-scale invasion, but bombing seemed one way of persuading the British to give up. The only reason he could see for their holding out was that the Luftwaffe had not hit them hard enough.

Goering became tired of patiently waiting for the capital city to beg for mercy. "We will never force them to their knees by bombing London," he told Hitler.

So the Luftwaffe began to broaden its attack and not to just random hits. People who lived outside the capital began to hear the sounds of the approaching bombers.

A heavy raid on Birmingham was successful enough to prompt the planning of another attack, this one on Coventry, just east of Birmingham.

Coventry was a strategic target for Germany. One of a number of British towns whose population had grown at more than five times the national rate during the 30s, it had a great deal of industry, which in wartime had been converted to produce war materials.

Although Coventry had experienced earlier raids, nothing would compare with the three days of hell that were about to begin.

10

COVENTRY

THE PRIME MINISTER finished his lunch with the minister of Shipping and made his way back to his office. A report from the Air Ministry was waiting for him. Intelligence had found that the Luftwaffe were about to launch their biggest attack of the war under the code name "Moonlight Sonata." The whole of the long-range German bomber force was to be employed in a massive raid on a British city. But which one? All signs pointed to an all-out attack on London as a reprisal for the British raid on Munich, but no one was certain.

In the early afternoon, London received reports that radio monitors set up in the south of England had begun to pick up Nazi transmitters. One after another, the radios of hundreds of bombers could be heard being switched on and tested.

Churchill decided to forgo his afternoon nap and make plans to leave London for his home in the country. Just as he was climbing into the car to leave Downing Street, the prime minister was handed a note. Intelligence had found that the German beams were crossing over the city of Coventry. Churchill immediately got out of the car. He wasn't going anywhere.

Although it was several hours before the first bombs were dropped, he did nothing to warn Coventry. Some weeks before, acting on a report from Ernest Bevan, a member of the war cabinet, he had instructed Coventry officials to strengthen defences, and he felt confident that the city could defend itself.

At 7 P.M. on Thursday, November 14, the first of Goering's bombers crossed the target area and began to release their bombs. For months the city had been the target of random raiders anxious to disrupt the lives of factory workers vital to the British war effort.

Joyce Whelan (now Hampson) was just one and a half miles from the centre of the city and a 20-minute walk from several car factories:

ADDED TO THESE were the textile factories, the gas works, a branch railway line, and goods yards, with the canal winding its way through the area. The houses were in terraced streets of two up and two down, outside toilets and small back gardens. There was only a narrow entry dividing us from the street behind ours.

Well, all the "old uns" kept telling us "youngsters" (I was 18) that Jerry would never find Coventry. "You see, we live in a hollow" (demonstrating this with their hands held in a V shape) "and we're right at the bottom." As no one had ever been higher than the cathedral spire we couldn't debunk this theory.

The first warnings came in July and August 1940. I can't remember the exact dates. Nothing happened, just the sound of an aircraft at odd times, which we were told was a Junkers 88. We got to know the sound very well.

Activity in the area quickened as everyone started to erect shelters. As there weren't enough to go round we shared with the neighbours. We all helped to dig holes.

We were sharing ours with a neighbour and friend named Templeman, whose back gate was opposite ours. Temp was crippled with arthritis and used a wheelchair but could manage to get into the garden. She had refused to be evacuated saying that bloody Hitler wasn't scaring her.

The firefighters used to help Temp to the shelter. She would painfully make her way along, holding the garden fence, and they would lift her down into the shelter.

One night the bombs got very close and everyone nagged her to evacuate, as she was risking the lives of the firefighters, who were men with young families.

Reluctantly she agreed to go the next day and her daughter, Kath, went with her to relatives in Macclesfield.

By now the bombing had reached our area, and my mother and my two young sisters left Coventry and joined Temp in Macclesfield. Just after this we had an incendiary bomb come through the roof of the house.

It did much damage before it could be dowsed, so afterward we could only use the downstairs rooms, throwing mattresses on the floor to sleep on.

We were all so tired with this constant lack of sleep, and we were getting some daylight raids, too. You never knew when to expect a warning apart from the regular night-time one.

It had been the practice in Coventry that when the clock struck 8 A.M. the factory gates would be slammed shut. Any worker arriving a minute late would be locked out and consequently lose a half day's pay. We could go into work after the midday dinner break, same procedure then at 1:30. So lots of people were oversleeping because of sheer exhaustion. Eventually these rules were dropped and we could go in to work at any time, so at least the raids did us some good as the practice was never resumed.

Came the night of November 14. A date stamped on every old Coventrian's brain. The moon was full and so bright you could read a paper by it. Such a beautiful sight for such a terrible night of death and destruction. I can never see a full moon now without remembering.

The sirens went at about 7 P.M. and we went down the shelter expecting the usual three or four hours. It was soon obvious that this was going to be more.

The planes came over wave after wave, and we could hear the whistle of falling bombs and the noise that incendiary baskets made as they spun around, sending their bombs in all directions, as well as the deafening noise of explosion and the smell of explosives.

Several times we felt the shelter shake, a tremor like a mild earthquake, I imagine. Once, the blast came through the shelter entrance, bending us over like saplings in a gale. We lost all notion of time, and still the moon shone on the town.

The wardens came round to see if we could take in some of the neighbours from the opposite side of the street. Six houses were down and the shelter on that side had got flooded. Two children of the Matthews family shared our shelter — Clive, he'd have been about eight, and his sister Myrtle, 10.

I don't know how long it was we sat holding their hands, trying to reassure them. They were very quiet.

Again the wardens came round to tell us that we had to evacuate the area, as an unexploded land mine had fallen across the main road, top of our street. It was reputed that a land mine could blow up a square mile, and later, seeing the devastation caused by a land mine in the Eagle Street area, I think we were lucky to be alive. I was told later that the Home Guard had spotted this object floating down by parachute and at first had thought we were being invaded and shot at it. Lucky they missed. Then when it did come down to earth (it was a coffin-shaped metal canister thing), they thought the Germans were dropping supplies for their invading troops. It was pulled and dragged to one side before someone recognized it.

We were all told to leave the shelters and to find somewhere else, and to leave the bottom of our street. As we went, people were talking of what had happened. A lady in the next street had been killed, and Betty Owen injured. Fred Kilburn was also dead, fighting the fires in town. The water mains were hit and they were having to let the fires burn.

We all got into the street — there must have been about a hundred people. I'll never forget how it looked. The six houses a pile of rubble, doors off, windows out, roofs off, lamppost leaning, when suddenly we heard the whistle of a bomb heading our way. We threw ourselves down on the rubble, a deafening explosion took place and, whoosh! Up shot flames higher than the houses, where the gas main had been damaged.

Someone was shouting, "Get out of here quickly. You're a sitting target." So we all started to run away — well, at least we tried, but had to climb over rubble and watch out for wires and the cables of the tram system, which were all down on the ground.

We reached Alfred Herbert's gates and the ARP there said the shelters were full to overflowing and to try the one at Foleshill Road. Clambering over rubble, we eventually reached it. All the time planes were still passing overhead and bombs were being dropped, but none as close as the one in our street, though.

In the road just outside the shelter was a small bomb crater with the front end of an ambulance tipped into it. We crowded into the shelter, and people in there asked us where we were from and what was happening. They told us that the police had popped in earlier and told them that the cathedral and all our city centre was bombed, burned and flattened. Other people kept coming in from other areas. Eventually it began to quiet down, and after quite some time someone went outside to see what was happening. He came back to say that it was getting light and he thought the raid was over. No all-clear sounded, since the sirens had all been damaged.

We crept out of the shelter to find a pall of smoke hanging over everywhere, the smell of burning and dust in the air. We slowly made our way back to our own area, climbing over debris and seeing houses that had been bombed or burnt since our flight past them in the night. Worn out, dejected and numb, we didn't know what to do, but like wounded animals instinctively crept back to our lairs.

A warden was still on guard. No, we couldn't go back, it was too dangerous. He didn't know where the rest of the Matthews family was. Not knowing what to do, my dad said he'd walk to work and meet me at the corner of the street again at six, and if we couldn't get into the house we could sleep in the shelter at Foleshill again.

As I look back now, it sounds ridiculous, but he was going to walk six miles to the Standard Shadow factory after the experience we'd had. But my dad had been out of work for years during the slump of the 30s. A skilled engineer, he couldn't even get a job sweeping up. So the idea of staying away from work never entered his mind.

He was also a very patriotic man and was on war work, and felt he'd be letting our lads down. That winter broke his health and he suffered with his chest for the rest of his days.

We heard that the King had come to see us and had climbed over the rubble and visited people. We were told not to go into town if possible, as the dangerous buildings were being blown up by sappers. We heard that Betty Owen had been found in a hospital in Stratford-on-Avon. As she had no identification on her and was too ill to talk, she was a "missing person" for nearly three weeks.

Our dead were buried in a mass grave, and even during the ceremony we had an air-raid warning.

Soldiers and gangs of men cleared the roads and did emergency repairs to the houses. At night it was like a ghost town, with empty streets and tarpaulins flapping in the breeze. Very eerie. Gradually we returned to a semblance of normality.

Brenda Mendenhall was 16 years old when the raid began. She was at the cinema with her father:

WE COULD HEAR the guns above the film, and when it was over we left to make our way home. We ran to a side street to one of the brick shelters outside a laundrette. We stayed there for about half an hour, and an old lady joined us. She was crying and clinging to me. Then a couple came in who knew the lady and they took her home.

Dad and I left the shelter and ran again up the road. The laundrette and the shelter were hit just as we left. Luckily no one else was in there. We ran to the common. There was a large underground shelter there, so we went into that and stayed there for some hours. Bombs were dropped on the common and even in the shelter we got terrific blasts which made many people scream and run farther along the shelter.

Dad and I just sat. I think we had had enough. We arrived home at 7 A.M. to find we only had the kitchen window broken, but no water, gas or electricity. I just got ready and went to work as usual.

Sid Lowe was one of a group of soldiers who found themselves stationed in Coventry, staying in a tent not far from the cathedral, during the city's dreadful blitz. The scene he witnessed will stay with him for the rest of his life:

EACH OF US had calmly decided to write a note of farewell to our loved ones. There was incessant bombing, and the town was still burning. Somehow I felt better to have written, sending my love. No one else was about, so I decided on a little walk, or see if I could find something to do to occupy my mind. Maybe I was a little bomb happy.

Then something most terrible was happening. Another kind of hell. Through the haze and the heat came several horses at full gallop, screaming. Dogs, too, trying to scramble on the backs of the horses. They passed me on either side as I stood rooted to the ground. Flames flickered on the horses' manes, tails on fire. One dog was wholly on fire, screaming in my ear as it brushed my shoulder trying to leap onto a horse.

How long I stood there I do not know. I felt I just could not move. As a little boy, I had heard a horse scream, having gone mad and having to be shot, but this was pure hell, another world.

It must have been near daybreak when I met up with a group of five or six Coventry lads. The bombing had ceased, and through the haze the cathedral loomed and a subdued cheer went up. It had survived!

Margaret Swaby was a qualified physiotherapist who lived in Skegness. Unable to get a job in a town that was extremely short of hospitals, she moved to Coventry to take a job:

I LIVED in the YWCA and spent many nights in the air-raid shelter, where I passed the time knitting. On November 16 several of us were invited to another YWCA hostel, also in Coventry, so we spent the evening and eventually the night there.

After several hours of much bombing one of our party had to spend a penny, and she was told there was a toilet just outside the shelter. We were a little surprised to hear a tinkle, tinkle, but were more surprised when someone who didn't know what it was cried out in alarm, "It's the church bells! The German paratroops have landed!"

Joy Bradbury's father was a Coventry policeman, whose night off coincided with the first brutal bombing of the city on November 14:

MY FATHER decided that our Anderson shelter was not really safe, but our next-door neighbour's had a cellar which was arched (originally a wine cellar). Therefore every night we used to sleep in the Joneses' cellar.

I was 11 and my sister Gillian two and a half. My mother had taken the wheels off her pram and she used to sleep in that. My mother and I used to sit upright all night because there was literally nowhere to lie down.

On that particular night the sirens sounded at about 7 P.M. The bombing started, horrific, 11 people being killed in a shelter (home-made) two doors from us. My father and my friend's father, who lived opposite, helped to carry out the bodies.

The all-clear went at 11. We came up to the living room and waited. Suddenly the windows all came in and there was a mad scramble to the cellar door which, incidentally, led off from the living room. Then the sirens went again. We had only one small anti-aircraft situated in Four Pounds Avenue, but that soon became red hot and went out of use.

Mr. Jones spent the night in the shelter timing the bombs, whilst my father and Mr. Turner toured the streets seeing what could be done. At 7 A.M. the all-clear sounded. Our house had the back blown in, and our old apple trees were all covered with bits and pieces, but I didn't realize they were bits of people from the home-made shelter.

At about 9 A.M. a soldier came by to borrow my mother's clothes-line to cut off the street because of unexploded bombs. A land mine was dangling between two entries, and my father and Mr. Turner got an old man out of one of the houses — he had slept through the lot!

In the event, my mother put Gillian in a basket which was on the front of her bike and I rode my "fairy cycle" through the centre of Coventry. We eventually arrived at my aunt's house in Nuneaten at 7 P.M., and my uncle calmly greeted me with, "When are you starting school, Joy?"

Many people were seen as heroes during the months of bombing. High on the list were hospital workers. Faced with the enormous task of caring for the sick and injured, they carried on with little regard for their own safety.

Irene Dore was a student nurse in a large training hospital when the war started. She left training school in 1940 and joined a Cardiff nursing agency. From there she was transferred to Coventry and hardly had time to settle in to her new surroundings when she found herself on night duty in a fever hospital (a hospital specifically for people, often children, with fever-producing diseases, such as measles):

ALL WERE CHILDREN with the exception of a pregnant mum. All patients had settled down for the night, and what a lovely calm evening it was. Despite the blackout there was a bright, full moon. Suddenly all hell broke loose. The air-raid sirens shattered our ears and almost immediately the bomber planes were overhead. The memory is so vivid I can see it clearly, so clearly, even now. In an adjoining field was an ack-ack unit with many balloons flying above. The bombs were now raining down, scaring the tiny tots, making some cling to our white aprons as we made our way to the air-raid shelters. A few yards from the ward entrance was a vast steaming crater. A land mine and part of the ward had collapsed.

Running back to the ward I could see some RAF men trying to control blazing balloons. Fires were raging all round. It was as if the lights had been switched on — you could have read a newspaper.

Patients were trapped in the ward debris, and several RAF men and medical staff were raising a heavy beam off the pregnant mum. An injection of morphine was called for. Another whistling bomb was heard coming for us, and the beam came down with a thud.

By now it was very light, not so many bombs were dropping, but planes were flying low and using machine guns. There was no returning gunfire from the ack-ack guns. They had quickly run out of ammunition.

I really cannot remember the following day. I do remember the following night. What little food we had was served on unwashed crockery. Baths that were still remaining held the only water we had. Patients slept on mattresses on the floor. I sat on the floor between, holding the hands of the children on each side.

For patients in hospitals, air-raid sirens were especially terrifying. Many were unable to move and relied completely on the nursing staff. Others were like Dennis Hill, a casualty of the November 14 bombing of Coventry, who was rushed to hospital for emergency treatment:

MY FRIENDS and I used to spend the evenings collecting shrapnel and caps from anti-aircraft shells — the biggest prize. Thus I was outside on this night, which was unique in that the bombing started early in the evening and, of course, as we did not know then, was going to be the heaviest air raid in England since the start of the war.

It was a cold crisp moonlit night. We became aware early on that it was going to be a heavier raid than usual, as I could hear voices in the darkness saying, "We are in for it tonight!"

Suddenly the whole street was lit up by incendiaries. I had been standing by the front door — my mother, sister and her two children sheltering underneath the stairs. My brother-in-law, an air-raid warden, wasn't home, and my father was out in the back garden.

I ran into the street, picked up a sandbag and threw it over an incendiary bomb which was lying in the gutter. That very second it exploded, I was thrown backward, and then realized that I could not see. Footsteps came running and someone said, "We must get him to hospital!" Then another voice said, "I'll get my car out and take him." Few people owned cars in those days.

The hospitals, fire engines and ambulances were all in the city centre, so we made our way into the city. To me it sounded like an enormous bonfire night. Bombs coming down made one kind of noise and anti-aircraft guns another. As we tried to make our way to Coventry and Warwickshire Hospital (which was bombed that night), a policeman stopped the car and said, "You'll never get through — all the roads are blocked. Your best plan is to go to Gulson Hospital." This was situated a short distance from the city centre.

After many detours we eventually arrived at the hospital. The raid by this time was at its height. All I could hear was clamour, crying and sobbing. I was handed over to a nurse and someone said, "This boy is blind." I can remember thinking, Will I be blind forever? And also that I wouldn't be able to collect all the shrapnel that would be lying around in the morning.

I was put into a bed and the last thing I heard was "The ward is on fire!" In the morning the ward was evacuated. I think it was a converted bus that took us to an emergency hospital in Rugby. My eyes had been sealed together by the blast and my eyebrows and the front of my hair singed off.

It was a week before my parents were able to find out where I was, as everywhere was chaos. When they came to see me I can remember my elderly father being annoyed that he had lost his best overcoat, which had been thrown over me, and my mother concerned about the ordeal of having to cook over the fire because there was no gas.

I was in hospital for two weeks and people would stop by the bed and say, "This little boy is blind," and I would lie there feeling quite heroic. I can remember falling in love with the voice of the ward sister, who was very kind to me. For quite some time afterward I would cycle over to Rugby to see her.

When I returned to school I was asked where I had been, and when I said in hospital no one seemed very interested. I found out later that one of my classmates had been killed that night.

Jean Watley was washing her hair when the sirens sounded. Her mother gathered up her personal papers, placed them in her handbag and, with her 14-year-old daughter, hurried to the nearest air-raid shelter, which was the local school:

WHEN WE GOT to the shelter there were crowds of people. We sat on wooden benches all night until seven the next morning.

When we got home most of the roof and a door were missing from our house. There was no gas or electricity, and our pet dog, Rover, had fled.

I went out searching for the dog. Many of the streets were sealed off, where time bombs were.

As I walked the streets looking for the dog, an emergency jeep stopped and soldiers gave me a lift halfway home. Rover eventually came home by himself!

When the sirens sounded, Jean Long, 21, thought it was just another nuisance raid:

I LIVED next to the canal and several small factories. My husband was abroad in the Royal Artillery. I had a small daughter. I was a post-woman and did first aid. That Thursday evening we had what we called a "bombers moon." We thought it was just another nuisance raid although Lord Haw Haw (the German propaganda broadcaster) said we would have a big raid by 10 o'clock. When we realized it was a big raid we went into the neighbour's Anderson shelter.

The bombs were raining down. We heard children screaming, then they stopped. We heard afterward that five children had been killed in a nearby shelter.

The hours dragged on as we waited for the inevitable bomb. The throb of the German planes, the bells of the fire engines. The ARP wardens came round for the first two or three hours to check. We were too frightened to even move. Four adults, one baby, one dog. We all huddled together waiting for death.

The sky was lit up by hundreds of fires. There was falling masonry, houses on fire, people screaming. For 10 hours it was a nightmare. We prayed for the morning to come.

Around 5 A.M. it all went quiet. We waited for the all-clear siren. It never came. We didn't dare go out. At about 7 A.M. we plucked up courage. The sky was blood red. No birds were singing. It was an uncanny silence. Fires were still raging where there was no water, and there was no electricity, no ambulances. Gas mains were fractured, smoke was thick.

One by one people came out, "if you were one of the lucky ones." We went across the road, picking our way through the rubble.

Our house looked all right. My mother pushed the front door and it fell off, and we could see straight through to the burning factory at the bottom of the garden. A bomb had blown out the back of our house.

We searched for belongings. All we found was the radio. It wasn't even scratched.

Everywhere was devastation. People were quiet. There was no panic — just weary, drawn pale faces with red-rimmed eyes. Clothes were soiled, some torn, yet in all that I never heard one word of condemnation. Everyone tried to help one another. The bond of friendship and caring was very strong.

Time and again there were reports of "ordinary people" doing extraordinary things. Jean Rees remembers:

MY FATHER was a hero of the bombings. He was one of two men who worked at the emergency mortuary in Hill Street and had to piece together bodies of all the unfortunate people who were killed and box them up. He used to raise his hat to them each night when he left.

Ron Patten was accustomed to what he called "run of the mill" raids on Coventry, and so was not concerned on November 14 when once again the sirens began:

MY FRIEND Den Burdett and I were regularly out in the streets putting out incendiary bombs either in houses or simply in the street. We both became adept at dismantling the charges from the incendiary bombs which had failed to explode. God knows what would have happened had any of these bombs been booby-trapped.

We rarely used the shelters, preferring to be in the thick of things, but on one occasion we had found a dud incendiary bomb, and after dismantling it, we decided we wouldn't keep it as a souvenir, as we had enough.

We thought that we would hand it in to the chief air-raid warden at the nearby shelter.

Although it was perfectly safe in its unassembled state, it caused trouble. As soon as we entered the shelter carrying the defused incendiary bomb, the women started screaming, "A bomb! A bomb! Get it out of here!" I had never encountered such hysteria. When we tried to explain that it was safe, the warden told us to put it in a bucket of water and take the bucket outside.

Amid shouts of abuse and more hysteria, Den and I quickly retired outside (with the bucket).

We decided that we would never again enter an air-raid shelter.

Thomas Parry was nine. His father was a senior air-raid warden who was off duty when the siren sounded:

AT APPROXIMATELY 9:30 P.M. all hell broke lose. The house next door received a direct hit. The lights went out, and brick and rubble were everywhere. The door which led under the stairs split into four pieces and was jammed solid by the weight of the masonry against it. All was silent, then we heard muffled voices. "Are you all right?" Dad and his colleagues began digging away and after what seemed like hours a torch light appeared and there was frantic movement to release all of us trapped.

After about three-quarters of an hour we managed to crawl though a hole into the front room that was. A man whose name

I never knew said, "I'll take this lad to my house." At which time he picked me up and away we went.

When we'd got about 100 yards, a bomb came down, a direct hit, on his house. He did no more than leave me lying on the pavement and went to see how best he could save his family. By this time my mum and dad were with me.

My dad said, "Let's get out into the county." So without further ado we started walking to what was considered a safe area (the fields on the outskirts of the city). We had gone about half a mile when we were dive-bombed. Dad then insisted we take shelter. The nearest building was the Co-Op Bakery, and the three of us went in there and under the tables.

The rats there were so numerous that they were running over our feet. Dad then decided that the place was unsafe and we should move on. We did, but because of the intensity of the bombing it took us half an hour to crawl 500 yards to the public house, in which we sheltered for the remainder of the raid.

About 6:30 A.M. the all-clear sounded and the three of us went outside to witness unbelievable sights. Tram lines standing up like soldiers, houses and shops demolished, roads blocked. An unexploded bomb on the corner of the street where we lived. Our own house partially collapsed, roof gone and a piece of tram line embedded in the bathroom that was.

At that moment Dad made a decision. We would all try and go to a friend's house in the neighbouring town of Nuneaten. So we started walking.

It's 11 miles and we walked all the way. Our friend was only too pleased to see us unscathed.

Coventry slowly began to lift itself out from the rubble. The full horror of the blitz and its effects were described in a letter written by Norman Bedford's Aunt Jonah to his mother in Yorkshire just 10 days after the November 14 raid:

MY DEAR ALICE,

Many, many thanks for your letter. I wonder if you received Len's postcard, for on the Friday following the raid, he and Cis went to Northampton till Sunday and he sent you a card to let you know that we were safe.

Alice, I shall never forget it as long as I live. My nerve has completely gone, I dread the dark, and the siren. The planes came over every minute, and they started on Green Lane at 7:45 P.M. I was sitting by the fire reading the paper, when the roar of guns and bombs was deafening, and George, Dad and I went to the back door to look. There were hundreds of flares dropped and tracer bullets going up, and the moon was brilliant. Dad couldn't understand why they dropped flares, for the night was like day. Suddenly he saw the roof on the corner house collapse, and we all drew back by the kitchen table, and we held each other in grim death, as the front door of the house blew in, and at the same time light, gas and water went off. We are still without it.

A mine had dropped in Beanfield Avenue, killed halfway up that street. The bus came to carry away the dead, and when it turned the corner into Beanfield, a bomb came down, and over the bus went. We had a bit of fire in the grate, and that blew out. George and Dad picked it up and threw it back, else we should have had the house on fire.

We all crouched in the hall, you know, between the two doors, sick with fright, and at 11 o'clock they dropped a mine on the corner of Harold's row. The blast from there blew the back of place in, and God, the way we clung together we thought our end had come. The roof fell over, and the fall of the plaster.... We really thought the house was falling on us.

There wasn't a minute's break for a solid 11 hours, and later on our guns gave out for want of ammunition, so of course the buggers had it all to themselves.

You wouldn't know Coventry. The whole town is down, nothing but mass rubble. All those beautiful shops, Boots, Flinns, the jewellers, all along there, down Smithford Street, Marks and Woolworth's, gone, not a shop standing anywhere. About 500 planes, one a minute. All factories are down, George's place is gutted, and even after more than a week, the place is burning in parts.

My darling, it was a nightmare. I pray to God that you never experience it.

At 6:30 the next morning the all-clear went, and I was as you have always seen me, in slacks and that jumper you made me. It has been a Godsend to me, and it is as black as hell — you wouldn't think it was pink — and I had on Dad's greatcoat. I waddled along to Harold's to see if he was all right. God, the sight that met my eyes. I'll never forget it. Nothing but charred ruins, and I thought they must be under it. I shed buckets of tears then and since, but they had just got out as the mine dropped by them. They ran under fire to a shelter in Woodside. Poor Harold has lost all.

Friday night it rained like hell, to add irony to our fate, but luckily in the morning we got all the beds downstairs and pushed everything downstairs up here. We have no bedrooms to sleep in, the roofs are gone, but George scratched his head on Saturday morning and said, "Charlie, we will have to do something to the roof," and he was wondering where to get a ladder when a bright idea struck him — get through the loft and work that way, so they did.

I wouldn't mind if we could get the wireless, and be able to look outside, but windows are boarded up. I feel like a prisoner, and it is such a job cooking on this little fire — my poor back. But I mustn't grumble, for I and ours have our lives, and up to the present I still have my reason. Alice, I think sometimes I shall go mad.

I am so tired. All my love to you and a big hug and kiss for Norman, and give my love to Horace. I hope he doesn't have to leave you.

Ever yours, Jonah xxxxxxx

Although Jonah decided to stay in Coventry, many felt the need to leave the city for the safety of the countryside. Shirley Goode was six years old and moved with her parents each night to a small village outside Coventry. Her father's job gave him an allowance for extra gasoline, which made it possible for the family to be mobile:

> MUM AND DAD found someone to let us have a room over a shop in a nearby village, so each evening we drove to the village to sleep away from the raids, and we returned the next morning.
>
> The day after the bombing of the cathedral Dad drove Mum and me to see the ruins, and as we came back via Hershall Common, we saw thousands of people clutching a few possessions and all walking away from town.

Barbara Smith lived with her family in Birmingham. Her father was a policeman and had been sent with a special force to Coventry to give what assistance he could:

> I WELL REMEMBER his return. He looked pale and haggard. Told us that he had not slept, eaten or even rested for three days; and when my mother said quietly, "What was it like, dear?" he answered, "Terrible," and burst into tears. At the age of 13 I had never seen a man cry.

As the German pilots made their way back across the Channel, they had good reason to be pleased. The Kampf Gruppe 100, specialists in finding and bombing targets at night, had left behind a city with nowhere to hide from the scorching heat. Coventry, a target so much smaller than London, had been easier to flatten. The 437 planes had dropped 56 tons of incendiary bombs, 127 parachuted land mines and 394 tons of high explosives. They had found little opposition from the RAF or anti-aircraft guns. Of the British night fighters that had made it into the air, only two found themselves close enough to the enemy bombers to attack. Anti-aircraft gunners claimed to have shot down one enemy plane.

11

THE DEADLY COLOURS OF AUTUMN

GOERING DECIDED to direct the Luftwaffe away from Coventry, a mistake, perhaps, because continued bombing of Coventry might have meant a devastating setback to the British manufacturing of war materials. Instead, within weeks of the one heavy attack, most of the factories in Coventry were functioning again. The Morris Motor Works, for example, which had had 600,000 square feet of roof torn off, was back to full production within six weeks.

A contented Goering had different ideas. Satisfied that Coven-try had been dealt a fatal blow, and convinced that the plan to attack other industrial areas of Britain was a good one, he decided to follow up the bombing of Coventry with attacks on Southampton and Birmingham, with side trips to the Midlands.

Living in Southampton, Emily Diminock had seen plenty of action. Much of the Battle of Britain had been fought directly overhead; locals had waved to paddle steamers making their way across the Channel to pick up British soldiers fleeing Dunkirk; and dozens of barrage balloons had found their way back to earth with the help of raiding Luftwaffe pilots. There was nothing the Germans could do that would stop Emily's wedding plans:

ON THE MORNING of my wedding day there was an air-raid warning before breakfast, so it we ate breakfast in our Anderson shelter, the all-clear went, and we went back into the house to erect the wedding cake. There was more gunfire, so we took the cake apart again and it accompanied us back into the shelter, where we left it for safety until our return from the church.

We were due at the church at 10 A.M., and my brother was to give me away. He had spent the night working at an aircraft factory at Hamble where he was an aircraft inspector, and the air-raid alerts meant he had to take shelter and the time of his journey home was tripled.

There was no time for nerves, pre-wedding or otherwise, because everyone had gone to church and I was the only one left to run around and help him get ready.

We did get to the church on time, but air-raid warnings interrupted the service and we had to go to the crypt for shelter. No photographs — no photographer or photographic materials were available. No honeymoon, either, although one had been arranged, but had we gone out of Southampton at that time we would not have been allowed back in. No one could come into Southampton then, except people vital to the war effort.

Wedding guests from Winchester travelling by bus were held up by soldiers boarding the bus. We bought strong walking shoes as it was freely rumoured that the civilian population of Southampton would be evacuated and we'd have to walk, but

Hitler's barges of troops on the other side of the Channel were bombed by the RAF, and he decided not to invade by sea.

I can still remember the eerie feeling when we went out of our back door when the night raids were very heavy and were confronted with a night sky lit up like daylight with Very lights hanging like candelabra over us and the incendiary bombs everywhere, the smell of burning and the sounds of crackling. We armed ourselves with garden spades and forks, plus the coal shovel and anything else we could find, and set about piling earth from the garden on the fire bombs and patting some out with the tools, but we were driven into the shelter when bombers came in over the flares and dropped high explosives.

We were joined by several unknown people who just came into our shelter shocked and dumb and went out again when the all-clear sounded. We never knew who they were.

Sheila Wright was seven when she was evacuated to Boscombe, in Devon, but by November 1940 she was back with her parents in Southampton. She remembers one night the sirens went:

I was running down the garden path. I looked up at the sky. It was bright with stars, and the beams from the searchlights were criss-crossing the sky. Then the guns began firing again and the noise was as bad as ever. I reached the opening to the shelter. I wanted to jump down into its safety but I just couldn't move. My mother was behind me telling me to get in, and then shouting at me. I could hear her, but still stood there frozen to the spot. My dad pushed my mother out of the way, picked me up and threw me into the shelter. Once I was inside I began to cry and shake.

My parents comforted me and my father explained that although I didn't think I was afraid I really had been too terrified to move.

Lorna Jones was working at her first job as a typist in her home town of Southampton. Her father was a part-time warden and during the winter of 1939 Lorna had begun doing night duty at the civic centre, manning a phone to take reports of incidents and passing on the information:

> AS THE RAIDS worsened we were sent to the public shelter under Holy Rood Church, where we had to waste many hours until the all-clear sounded. My mother and I were coming back from lunch one day when without any warning we saw a formation of enemy planes approaching. We dived for the back door, hoping to make it to the Anderson shelter. The sunny day had turned to night by the bombs already falling and the debris thrown up.

Doris Hayman (now Bird) was 17 and living in Sale, near Manchester, at the time of the blitz:

> IT WAS impossible to sleep or feel safe even in the Anderson shelter below ground, so most of us muffled up against the cold and stayed outside. My father and I stood on the cobbled stones in Britannia Road and watched in horror as Sale Town Hall burned.
>
> The clock, the beautiful dance floor and the whole top floor disintegrated. I was absolutely terrified and trembling. I clutched my new black court shoes to my bosom and decided that if I was going to heaven, then my shoes were going with me.

The Birmingham house where Bryan Savage lived backed onto the railway line to London. Her father, a veteran of the First World War, spent three nights a week fire watching at his office in the centre of the city and spent the remaining nights at home. She remembers the night of the infamous 13-hour November raid on Birmingham:

> MY FATHER was a man with life strictly timetabled, and each night when at home he would have his supper in the living

room and listen to the midnight news on the radio whilst eating, despite the air raids. The rest of our family would always go into the cellar.

Exactly on the stroke of Big Ben's midnight chime on the night of the big raid, the whole house shook, following a tremendous explosion. My brother, sister and I rushed up the steps from the cellar to the ground floor, through the bricks, broken furniture and choking dust into the living room. There we found Dad unconscious, his face in the supper dish, and festooned by the washing that had been hanging on the clothes airer (it was a line fastened to the living-room ceiling and moved up and down by a rope pulley).

The bomb had exploded just behind the houses on the other side of the road, and the subsequent blast had brought down our substantial chimney, which then crashed through the ceiling — and brought down the clothes airer. My father had caught the full force of its cast-iron frame and was knocked out.

Marion Sutten was 15 and living in Birmingham:

I RAN to the window as the first German aircraft came over and saw the explosions of three bombs. These were only small bombs, but of course everyone was horrified and flocked in hundreds the next day to see the damage. One house was split into two, and the husband and wife landed one in the front and one in the back garden. The St. John's Ambulance ran the ambulances that day, and a friend on duty that night told me of her horror in finding that the man had a leg missing. She was greatly relieved when he said, "Don't worry, lady. I always leave it in the corner of the room when I go to bed."

R. W. Wright had taken shelter in the cellar of his Birmingham butcher shop. It had a tiled floor, a tap, drain and, most important, three exits:

I WAS by myself and frightened to death, of course, but hungry, so I was busy cooking a lamp chop, which I had dangling on a bit of wire in front of an electric fire with a tin on the floor to catch the fat. A loaf of bread and a bottle of beer and, oh, a bottle of tomato sauce.

It was about 8 P.M. I hadn't quite got to my chop when our bomb fell. It fell through the roof, straight through four storeys and down into the cellar where it hit the wall, deflected at an odd angle and came to rest underneath where I was sitting.

The cellar shook like a boat. The lights went out and so did I, pretty quickly, I can tell you. I found an air-raid warden who found the police who found the AFS who found the bomb-disposal squad. All these people, one after the other, I guided down to the cellar to view the mess and the hole down which the bomb had disappeared. The conclusion? A delayed-action bomb. Everyone was kicked out who lived anywhere near. A rope was stretched across Bryton Road and Edward Road and no one could go into this forbidden area.

All that night the bombs kept falling. I spent most of the time hiding behind the sandbags piled up in front of the library.

When morning came I was tired out, as you can imagine, and in despair wondered what the hell to do. There was the shop, full of meat and no one allowed to go near. By this time my staff, Albert Burford, whom we used to call Skylark, his wife, Dorothy or Doll, and his half brother, John, arrived. Well, I remembered that about half a mile down the road was an empty shop that used to sell fish. So I asked him if we could get the key, which he soon did.

The neighbours supplied hot water and we soon cleaned up the shop. Then we went back to the road barrier and asked Inspector Swift to allow us to go into our shop and get supplies.

"Certainly not," he said. "The slightest tremor could set off that delayed-action bomb and blow up half the district."

Well, anyway, we decided to take a chance and went down Clifton Road around the back, climbed over a few walls and we were in. That is, Skylark, John and me. Frightened to death, we were. We sneaked about on tiptoe. We didn't even start the van, but pushed it toward the fridge and loaded up with everything like knives, saws and scales, and I don't know what else.

Then we carefully opened the yard gates and pushed the van into the road and down to the barricade where Inspector Swift was having a fit.

Well, he didn't like to tell us to take it back, so we strung a notice on the rope which told anyone who wanted to know that Wrights, the butcher's, was now temporarily transferred to Mosely Road where it would be business as usual.

On Tuesday afternoon I suddenly remembered our little dog. We had a small Pekingnese bitch named Sandy and she had a couple of pups about as big as duck's eggs. So back I went and nipped into the shop. There was a side door to the living quarters which were behind and over the shop. So I opened the door and gave a nice soft whistle and out trotted Sandy and her two pups.

All the people watching cheered. You'd have thought we'd won the war.

Soon after this, the bomb-disposal squad arrived and started digging. I told them where I thought the bomb was, but they wouldn't listen to me and faithfully followed the path the missile had made, making a nice tunnel, properly shored up and everything. It took a long while to reach our bomb, I can tell you. Till the next morning, in fact. Then the brave soldiers dragged the thing back until it rested on the floor of the cellar, underneath some iron doors which opened onto the pavement above.

The next thing was to tie a rope around the bomb and trail it up the stairs, over the pavement and across the road where the rest of the squad, about eight or 10 of them, were standing.

I can remember them gathering around like a tug-of-war team under the leadership of the sergeant who stood by and shouted, "Heave!" which they did with some success, too.

"Heave!" shouted the sergeant again, and the bomb moved up another foot or two. All the people watching stood very quiet and fascinated, waiting to see the bomb appear up from the cellar and onto the pavement. "Heave!" shouted the sergeant, and there it was at last. Just peeping over the pavement edge. "Heave!" shouted the sergeant once more and they did. Then the rope broke. All the tug-of-war team went arse over tip into a great pile of arms and legs. On the other side of the road our bomb, which would explode at the slightest tremor, fell back down the stairs with a very satisfied "thud" to the floor again.

Well, all this was too much for the audience, who all burst out into spontaneous laughter and applause. The soldiers picked themselves up with sheepish grins, dusted themselves down, tied the rope together into a great big bow and started again. After several good heaves the bomb at last was dragged out. All 500 pounds of it, and rolled down the pavement into the gutter.

The lieutenant then sent all the squad, except the sergeant, away. The barriers were moved another 50 yards up the street, and we were moved, too, of course. Then, believe it or not, the sergeant sat astride the bomb and attacked it with a hammer and chisel. After a good few bangs he threw the hammer down and let it be known that the thing was harmless.

It was a delayed-action bomb, but the fuse was a dud. The rope barriers were taken away and all the crowd gathered around to congratulate the soldiers and view the bomb. By this time the hat was being passed around and a goodly sum was collected and passed to the lieutenant and his crew.

We hurried into the shop to try and get things shipshape and start up business again.

In the devastation there was always something that escaped. Beryl Room emerged after the 13-hour blitz on Birmingham to find that the whole street had been destroyed — almost:

AT THE END of the raid we went to look for where our house had been and there among the debris stood our piano with hardly a scratch on it. Also the family cat was sitting on top of it, having a wash!

Sheila Freeman had been working as an inspector of munitions and had left to live in a small village outside Exeter. At 8 A.M. a German bomber came sweeping out of the sky and dropped a bomb that hit the house and completely destroyed one wall:

MY LANDLADY was so annoyed that she forgot all about her safety and ran into the road shaking her fist up at the bomber saying, "You bastard! We haven't even finished paying for that house yet!"

Millicent Bransom was 10 when the war started, and living on the Isle of Wight. During a family visit to Portsmouth with her two sisters the warning sirens began to wail:

AS WE CROWDED into the shelter together with an aunt, uncle and cousin, it was soon apparent that this was a more than usually heavy raid. Whenever my uncle removed the door of the shelter, the sky glowed an angry red and the noise was almost as bad as Dad had always warned us to expect.

Uncle and Dad made frequent sorties above ground to check that no incendiaries had caught the house.

It was not until years later that they revealed they had spotted a stationary ammunition train on the main London-Portsmouth railway line, which ran the other side of the garden wall — literally only yards from the shelter!

I can clearly remember my mother agonizing that she had left our three new winter coats upstairs, and every time Uncle ventured out Auntie would say, "Put the kettle on for a cup of tea, Jack." Uncle's reply was unprintable.

Although Bristol had experienced air raids, it was not until the last weeks of November that the city felt the full force of a Luftwaffe attack. Olive James (now Perry) was 14 and living with her family in the south part of the city:

EVERY NIGHT we were out of our beds and under the stairs, Kath, my stepmother, nursing her baby in her arms. On one of these raids my gran's house next door was alight, her bedroom burned out by incendiaries, and the neighbours formed a bucket chain which saved the rest of the house and the whole block of houses.

Dad was on fire watch, and when the raids got really bad, he shouted to my sister and myself to get up and keep away from the windows, as shrapnel was falling like rain. The noise was the thing I remember. The guns pounding, and mobile guns going up and down the road. Then a cheer would be heard and a call to see the German plane that had been hit, smoke trailing, as it plunged to the ground.

Dad came in one night when he was on fire watch and told us a young man, just married, had been killed by bomb blast. He had lain in the road when he heard the stick bombs coming down instead of the grass verge where Dad and others were, and had died without a mark on him.

The Anderson shelters were put in the back gardens now, and Dad put wooden bunks and duck boards on the concrete floor of ours, with an oil lamp for lighting. It all looked cosy.

One night he came running up the stairs telling us the raid was getting bad and we must get up and go into the Anderson shelter. We looked in, but with Dad and Kath and the baby there wasn't much room. We went into the garden next door and lifted the sack across the opening. Gran and Uncle Bill were sitting in deck chairs with the frost glistening on the floor.

This was enough for us and we decided then and there that we would take our chances under the stairs or sit by the fire grate in our easy chairs. We never went into an Anderson shelter again.

I was visiting my maternal grandmother in Bristol when a major raid started. I was ready to get the 6 A.M. bus into the centre of Bristol when Gran asked me to get the later bus and stop and talk for a while. The sirens went between 6 and 6:30 P.M. The buses stopped running and I had to stay at Gran's.

As the night wore on things got worse. There were bombs falling all around. My uncle George, who had been in the First World War, was in and out of the house talking to the fire watchers and ARP men, and coming indoors to tell us of the latest direct hits. The noise was terrific and Gran gave me some cotton wool to put in my ears. Purdown Percy, the huge anti-aircraft gun, was firing most of the time and adding to the noise of the explosions from the bombs.

The all-clear sounded in the early hours of the morning. Uncle George walked me into town as it was a Monday and my job at the tobacco factory was near the centre. When we walked under the underpass of Templemead station we came into Victoria Street. What I saw was devastating. Buildings burning, factories just a mass of twisted girders with walls collapsing, and water and gas pipes fractured. Fire hoses all over the road. Temple Church was blazing with long flames reaching right through the fallen roof. I wondered if the factory had been hit. As we neared the rear entrance, there were shouts of foremen to stay clear of walls and unexploded bombs. There was a crater in the road caused by a land mine. Most of the buildings were gutted by fire.

The factory was somehow intact except for broken windows and the electricity cut off.

The Bristol I knew — Castle Street, Old Market — was gone overnight, but St. Mary Redcliff stood out against the rubble and burnt-out shops. Our chemist shop had the plate glass blown out, but the glass shelves still had bottles of perfume and medicines undamaged.

The dray horses at George's Brewery were injured and no one could get to them because of the damage. Their cries were pitiful to hear.

I feel that Gran's asking me to get the next bus saved my life, as I would have been caught in the target area when walking from Old Market to my bus at Princess Street.

Dad found the fin of an incendiary bomb in the cavity wall, causing a damp patch. He also had a new toilet pan fitted in the bathroom, because a stray bomb had dropped in front of the house, causing a pavement slab to crash through the roof and smash the pan in half. As Dad said with a smile, "Good job nobody was sat on it at the time."

Wendy Gibbs was living in Bristol when the sirens went, and she, her mother and four sisters headed for the Anderson shelter at the bottom of their garden:

NEXT DOOR they were rather posh, so they had a brick shelter made.

My father was in the Home Guard, so had not joined us in our shelter. We were all awake, as we couldn't sleep, and suddenly we heard this plane. Mum said, "It's a bloody plane coming down." We all got up and tore back the curtains on the shelter door to look. It was not only a plane coming down but a parachute, too. As he floated down he got closer and closer and suddenly landed on the roof of the brick shelter next door. It was a German pilot, so my mother said, "There's nobody about so I suppose I'll have to do it. She grabbed a pitchfork and a broom and marched out to the garden next door and stood at the bottom of the shelter and, facing the pilot, said in a loud voice, "You're under arrest. Put your hands up!" She was fantastic.

He surrendered to my mother and gave her his parachute. She quickly threw it into the shelter before the Home Guard came to take him away. The next day she dyed the chute yellow, and two weeks later two little girls went off to school dressed in bright yellow dresses.

Mary Birch was 13 in November 1940, and she was busy washing dishes at her home in Bristol:

AS THE SIREN started I went to say, "Oh, no, not again," when all hell broke loose. We shot under the stairs, followed smartly by the cat, and remained there until the all-clear.

I lived on the outskirts of the city and my route went mainly past quiet fields. School was almost empty. There were about three boys and myself in my class. No work was done until we had history with the senior mistress, our last lesson. She demanded our homework. Mine had been done on Friday under mother's eagle eye. The boys tried to slide out of it, saying, "There was a blitz!"

Gwen Adams was living in Bristol with her mother, three-year-old brother and two aunts, who were getting away from the London bombing:

THE NIGHT of November 24 was the first big blitz on Bristol, when most of the centre area was wiped out. We went to bed to be woken by air-raid wardens about one hour later. They said we had an unexploded bomb in the road outside. We dressed quickly and set off walking to a school about two miles away where there were hundreds of others who had been bombed out. My brother and I found a corner of floor while my mother and aunts set to helping with food and drink. In the morning we went outside and walked toward the Bedminster area, passing some houses where some ladies were at their gates talking.

One lady asked what we were doing. Obviously my mother must have explained. This lady (I don't remember her name) said, "Come in and use my front room for as long as you want it." We stayed there for four days while the bomb near our house was dealt with. It sums up the spirit of the times. Strangers who helped out other strangers.

Mrs. M. Pennock arrived back at her home in Swansea after spending an evening walking with friends. The siren went and they took shelter under the Guild Hall for the night:

WHEN I EVENTUALLY got to our street I could see straight-away that our house had had a direct hit. Only my mother and brother had been there, but luckily they went to the Anderson shelter. My mother tried to shield my brother when the bomb fell and got some shrapnel in her back which nearly pierced her lung. It was never removed and caused her death in the end. I was lucky in a way, because I would never go to the shelter, and most of the roof of the house fell on the bed in my room.

Anyway, the wardens took me to the house where most of the survivors were all crammed in one room. My mother and my brother were there with a lot of bombed-out people, and in the far corner was a friend of ours who had gone into labour and was having her baby. It was all such a nightmare. I had only got married in the July, so I not only lost my home and nearly lost my family, but I lost all my wedding presents, clothes, the lot, but was so thankful that my mother and brother were saved.

Twenty-year-old Betty Baxter was living in Swansea. She was visiting a sister who had given birth to a baby that day:

THEY KEPT a hotel, so we carried her downstairs, went to the bar and all buried our heads under the bench seats. I don't know why, but we felt we'd be safer doing that. We hadn't got used to the shelter at that time.

A favourite uncle was taken short with shock. He was in the outdoor loo when another bomb was whistling down. He came running in, and you've heard the saying, "Never let your braces dangle." Well, that happened to Uncle and we weren't sure if we didn't prefer the bombs to his company.

It's reassuring to regard times of disaster as times when people are kind, considerate and go out of their way to help their neighbour. But unfortunately this is not always so, and goods suddenly lying around unclaimed proved too much of a temptation for some.

Peggy Parker had three small children and was bombed out in December 1940:

We had all saved up and got the children their Christmas presents, and looters came in the night and took everything. It was heartbreaking, because we could not afford any more. Their fingers should have dropped off, but they did it to most houses, not only mine.

Henry Barnes was home on leave from the RAF during a heavy raid on Hull. His father's grocery and beer off-licence shop was completely destroyed:

AS SOON AS DAYLIGHT dawned, the inevitable happened — looters! A policeman was sent to guard the goods and he turned out to be the father of the girl I was married to. My own mother and father came to our house at 3 A.M. and found us crouching in the Anderson shelter. Their first words were "We've lost everything. All we have are the few clothes we're wearing."

As daylight came my father said, "Will you go to the shop and see if you can rescue the cash?" I knew where the cash bag was kept — in a fixture no more than about three feet from the ground. I arrived to find this bit of wall still standing. I moved some rubble, managed to get my hand into the fixture and there it was. Intact! Every penny. The looters had missed it.

Connie Brown (now Blunsum) had been out to an ARP lecture and had just returned to her home in Paddington, London, at about 8:45 P.M. when the siren sounded:

WE COULD NOT have an Anderson shelter because we were a corner house. About 9 P.M. there was a noise like a train rattling down, then a shrill whistle and a bang, then we went up in the air and down again. I did not lose consciousness and was covered by rubble and pinned down by a dining chair, which had lost its seat and was over my shoulders. We remained buried till about 5:30 A.M. the next day.

A 500-pound bomb had fallen and exploded in the back garden. My house was a complete loss, and the houses on either side were in various stages of demolition. Four people were killed and 19 injured. My father was a policeman on war reserve, as was our next-door neighbour. The neighbour and his wife were found dead at their meal table.

The people in the downstairs flat had just brought their daughter home from Exeter where she had been evacuated. She went to lie down for a rest and her body was found the next day. The fourth death was a young baby from the upper flat next door, whose mother had flung herself over the cradle to protect her. The mother suffered two broken legs. The baby died.

I can remember the sounds of men digging and then calling to us after what seemed ages. When the rescue gang got nearer they told us to cover our heads. I put my arms up, and a brick smashed into my elbow, and my face and hair were covered in glass. The gentleman from the ground floor was injured beside me, but we couldn't move to help each other. Then the rescuers said they were going to lower flasks of water on a rope. I managed to catch one but could not get my head back to drink because the back of the dining chair made putting my head back impossible.

Eventually I was released, and to add insult to injury the man assisting me said, "You'll be all right now, son." Not very flattering for a 19-year-old girl.

We lost our home and all our belongings. The hundredweight of coal we'd got in for the winter was looted, along with some unbroken movable objects and clothing.

A few days after a bomb had destroyed her family's Lewisham home, Barbara Grant (now Dear) and her father went back to see what they could salvage of their belongings:

THE BUILDING was unsafe and we were not allowed other than the most perfunctory of searches — although we managed to find a few documents and light household goods. Remarkably, however, someone had managed to get in, because everything of value, including bedding and furniture, had been looted. We were numb with sorrow and hung on to each other and cried.

Such a contrast to the people who had been so kind to us after the bombing. Not all Londoners were so honourable and willing to help the unfortunate.

Mary Richards (now Brown) lived with her parents close to Coventry, and after constant air raids her father decided it would be a good idea to visit relatives in the small town of Bedworth for a few days:

AS LUCK WOULD HAVE IT we went to stay with them the very night before the blitz on Coventry. The next night we were woken by the dreadful noise of German aircraft passing over.

Two days after the blitz my older brother and some friends went over to our Coventry home on their bikes to try to bring back some of our possessions (clothes) and to find out the extent of the damage. Well, the house had lost its roof, all the windows had gone, all the ceilings were down and the furniture damaged and pottery all smashed.

I remember the one thing that hurt my mother the most was that someone (who was very expert) had entered our house and taken about two feet of bedding off the front of her sideboard. It had been done very neatly.

A lot of looting had already taken place by this time, and many of my clothes, toys, and our household possessions had been taken. At this stage of my life I couldn't believe that others would enter someone else's house and take things away.

Weather conditions during the beginning of December forced the German bombers to stay home. It was the beginning of a period when the air raids would cease being be a nightly occurrence — at least in most of England.

The German planes still found time for London. The attacks continued, leaving houses in some areas flattened into piles of bricks, which formed new playgrounds for local children. The houses that remained standing in the bombed locations suffered shortages of gas and water as burst mains spilled their contents along glass- and rubble-strewn roads. People could be seen each morning salvaging what little they could and piling the stuff on carts to be wheeled off to friends', neighbours' or local rest centres.

The number of homeless in London had reached 250,000 before the end of October. After one particularly heavy night of bombing, one-fifth of the homes in the London area were without gas or water.

The sufferers looked to the government for help, but dealing with bureaucrats only seemed to add to their problems. This lack of help came as no surprise to the poor, who knew that even when improvements were approved by government officials, they seemed to take forever to be implemented. It wasn't until the end of November, for instance, that the Treasury finally agreed to help with the cost of solving the problems of the homeless, and public shelters were at last provided with electric lighting and toilet facilities.

News that electric lights were being supplied to many shelters soon became a talking point in St. George's Buildings. For almost 70 years residents, now including Nell and her neighbours, had been reaching up with a match to light a gas mantle. The news was enough to make Alf jokingly suggest that they move house and home to one of the ugly red brick surface structures with its wooden seats and cold cement floor.

In October 1940 Hugh Dowding was retired from his post as Chief of Fighter Command, and Air Marshal Sholto Douglas took over. Many felt that Dowding had been treated shabbily, for, with an untried army of professional and amateur pilots, he had held the legendary Luftwaffe at bay, and forced them to attack only under cover of darkness.

The German bombers, meanwhile, had a new form of navigational aid: a system of special transmitters that sent radio beams across to England until the sound in the earphones signalled that they were over the target. In the attacks on London this was hardly necessary, however, as the target could be seen for miles. The sky glowed with leaping flames and the sweep of searchlights trying to catch a plane in their beams.

The British night fighters did not give the raiders a problem. They'd tried to use the twin-engine Blenheim, an aircraft designed for daylight action, but after a number of mechanical failings it was put to one side. The ack-ack, although a wonderful morale booster with its constant banging and puffs of smoke high in the sky had little success, either, and rarely was an enemy plane seen to suffer a direct hit. As well, the firing of many of the larger guns broke most of the windows in the houses nearby. The shrapnel they sent back to earth caused almost as many casualties as the bombs being dropped by the planes.

The various noises heard during an air raid encouraged all manner of guesswork as to what weapons the Germans were using.

Monica Harris (now O'Brian) had a younger brother who kept white mice:

DURING A PARTICULARLY heavy raid they escaped when a blast broke open their cage door. Our family was in the Anderson shelter when suddenly these little white creatures were running down into the shelter.

"My God!" said my mum. "Now they're dropping white mice!"

Throughout the autumn, the Luftwaffe raids continued on London. H. F. Dobson lived with his mum and dad in Essex, just a mile from the Thames. At the height of the blitz the Germans had hit the oil tanks at Purfleet just a few miles down the road:

MY MUM WAS so scared that she wouldn't let my dad report for Home Guard duty. Eventually his commanding officer came round to the house to find him. We were all down the shelter in the garden. The commanding officer told my dad he would have to go, as they were expecting to be invaded that night.

Mum was crying for him not to leave us, so Dad said to Mum, "Look. I've got a bottle of whisky indoors. I'll leave that with you, Eileen, and every time a bomb drops close, you have a swig of it."

So off he went with the officer. Well, in the morning at about seven, Dad popped his head in the shelter doorway and said, "Are you all right, Eileen? Let's have a swig of that whisky. I've had a hell of a night."

Mum pointed to the empty whisky bottle and said, "I don't care if Hitler himself walks in here." She was as drunk as a lord.

Peggie Hickson had spent nearly a year driving a double-decker bus that had been converted into a mobile canteen for the National Fire Service. She remembers the sinking of the *Marchioness* at Southwark Bridge:

WE HAD BEEN ALERTED to go to a big fire near the bridge and I had to park the bus as near to the water as possible. To our horror we could see a land mine caught by its white parachute on one of the iron pikes swaying gently backward and forward. We were all terrified that it would hit the bridge. The bomb-disposal men did a superb job detonating it, and eventually we were sent to Warren Street.

The courage of the firemen was fantastic. Never complaining and giving us a cheer when we arrived. In the early morning we returned to the fire station, driving through the streets of London to be flagged down by city gents waving umbrellas, thinking it was their bus to get to work. We thought this was very funny, especially since I'm only five foot four and in those days weighed only seven stone and had to sit on cushions to see over the driving wheel.

Elsie Swann lived with her parents in North London during the bombing raids of 1940. Every night she would dash home from the office, eat a meal, get washed and changed into pyjamas, slacks and jumper, ready for the night:

FOR THESE THREE MONTHS my mother and I slept on a bed made up on the floor underneath the staircase of our house, and my two sisters slept underneath a heavy billiard table. My father, who was a veteran of three major battles in the First World War, insisted on sleeping upstairs.

Sometimes the raids were so long the all-clear had not sounded when it was time to go to work the next morning, but nobody ever thought of being late for work.

Dorothy Hicks was working as a telephonist in the House of Commons:

OUR SWITCHBOARD was at the top of one of the turrets. In my lunch break I was standing by the window when a stray fighter plane made a dashing run for it up the Thames. Thinking it was one of ours, I opened the window wide to cheer him on. He opened fire on me!

Nan Eaton had said goodbye to her little 12-year-old girl, who was being evacuated, and as she headed home thought about how to fill her empty hours. She finally found a job and ended up working seven days a week. She was living with her husband in a tall Victorian house in London when the bombing started:

MY HUSBAND wanted me to go down the tube to shelter every night. I was there when the West End caught on fire.

In the morning all trains and buses had stopped. I had to get to work somehow. We never thought of not going, even if we had been awake all night. After sheltering all night we still had to come out and face the daylight raids. I made my way to Marble Arch in the hopes of getting a bus to work. I went through the arch and watched some men roping off a bomb with red flags when someone shouted. A man jumped on my back and pushed me down and shielded me from the blast. He had his jacket sleeve ripped off and I had miraculous escape. I was covered in rubble, my hands, chin, knees, nose and forehead raw and bleeding.

I saw in a flash a horse and cart going up in the air. A man on a bicycle and the men roping off the bomb all lying in the road. I think they were all dead.

The man who had helped me looked ruefully at his jacket sleeve, asked if I was okay and went off and never told me his name. I have often wondered who he was and if he survived it all.

I was now shaking with shock and worried because I had no more stockings. I could see my bus coming, and I ran for it as fast as my now shaking legs could carry me. On the bus was a man I worked with. He was shocked at the state I was in and advised me to go home and make some tea and he would tell them at work. We always had a roll-call every morning and anyone not answering was presumed bombed out or dead.

When I got home I had no front door. It had been blown off. After this we decided to move into a little house in the next road, one with a cellar.

Sunday mornings we spent on a bomb site at the bottom of our road being taught by real firemen how to put out fires in houses. They erected a shed and piled old furniture in it, then set it alight. We had to stand in line and pass buckets of water to put it out. All this in between trying to cook the dinner.

Henry Baggott was out fire watching:

THE GERMANS had been dropping bombs for quite a while when suddenly flares were dropped directly above. I looked around but could not see any of the others, so I went to a brick shelter where we kept our equipment for dealing with incendiary bombs. I pushed the door open and found the other men inside. One of the men said, "Come in quick." Just as I said no, I heard the whine of a bomb falling. I dropped between both shelters, kept my chest off the ground and breathed through my teeth. Then from the corner of my right eye I saw a shower of sparks and heard a grinding noise. Everything then seemed to be hitting me. I found myself buried up to my thighs in the crater. The men in the shelter, including a 14-year-old, were all killed.

Doris Collier (now Jaye) was 14 and had returned to London after being evacuated. She and her father watched a German aircraft being shot down:

MY FATHER and I ran to have a look. I pulled on my slacks, but in my haste they were back to front, so I ran down the road holding my trousers up. I was most disappointed at only seeing a pair of flying boots, as we hated the Germans so much I wanted to see a body.

Honor Kenyon was a schoolteacher who lived close to Marble Arch, in London:

A WHOLE BLOCK of evacuated old homes in Eastbourne Terrace running along the west side of Paddington Station had been turned into a hostel for all ranks of the service where they could get a good meal and bed for a very small sum.

The hostel was manned by volunteer workers, and my stretch was from 10 P.M. to 2 A.M. each day. After a particularly bad night and a full day's work, I felt so tired that I rang the supervisor and cried off for one night.

That night, at about 1 A.M., a land mine dropped in Eastbourne Terrace and destroyed the entire block.

I then joined the staff of an officers' club in Westminster. One day, Clark Gable arrived for a meal. He sat down at one of the tables and immediately produced a comb and combed his hair.

Kitty Steel lived in London and served the first year of the war as a nurse in a clinic that served as an air-raid shelter. She asked to transfer to the buses:

WELL, THE PAY for nurses was two pound, 10 shillings, and a bus conductor four pound, 18.

My daughter, Molly, was expecting her first baby and decided to go to Scotland and stay with her husband's mother. We received a letter from the Lewisham Council that if she did not come back to occupy the house she had left they would take it over for people who had been bombed out. So she came back. One night the warning went and a bomb dropped next door.

Fortunately my daughter was down below in a shelter. A neighbour called out, "Are you all right, Molly?" and Molly said, "Yes! My door key is under the front doormat." The neighbour called back and said, "Your front door is on top of your stairs, Molly."

Betty Wells lived in Fulham, southwest London, with three aunts, a great-aunt and a sister:

MOST NIGHTS during the blitz in our Anderson shelter my great-aunt was always coming home with gadgets to enable us to boil a kettle in the shelter. One day she bought home something resembling a cocoa tin with a night-light in it, and we took turns holding the kettle over it. I cannot remember what came first — the all-clear or the tea.

Eileen Horrocks lived and worked in London:

THE CITY had been bombed mercilessly. After one particularly bad night, the morning at last dawned.

Arriving at the entrance of Debenham and Freebody, where I worked in the basement office, I was very moved to see our office cleaner on her knees, washing the small-paned glass pavement lights.

As the Christmas season approached, people could remember the bright decorations of years past, which only made the blackout seem bleaker and more oppressive.

Movies and concerts were still very popular, and most people went in the afternoons in order to get home before the blackout. But even losing oneself in a movie or concert didn't always provide escape from the awful reality of war.

Mary Scott had booked to see a charity concert on Sunday, December 22, 1940. She writes:

I'VE NEVER FORGOTTEN that Sunday night. The show had just started when an incendiary bomb came down and the curtains caught fire. The manager was in one of the circle boxes directing the stirrup pump down, and then the safety curtain was lowered. Stanley Tudor started playing the organ and everyone joined in. There was no panic. We were all led out to a brick air-raid shelter.

My friend and I decided to try to walk home. The planes came back and gunfire was heavy. As usual the bombers seemed to be following the Thames. There was a factory on the corner and we thought we would shelter there. There was a night watchman in there who seemed to be alone. I think he was pleased to see us. He had an old round iron fire, glowing with red cinders, and he gave us a cup of tea.

After about an hour (we sat and talked together and told him how bad things were out there) the raid had quieted down a little, and we decided to try to get home.

It was hop, skip and jump and shelter, and then we ran. We used to go down the cellar belonging to the family opposite and that's where we headed. When we got there I called, "Let us in quickly!" They helped us down. They were all relieved to see us, but my friend couldn't get home until the morning. Her parents were frantic — none of us had telephones, though I don't think they would have worked, anyway.

When morning came I walked my friend home. We had to do a detour because the shortcut, an iron bridge over the river, was bomb damaged and useless. That meant we had to pass the factory where we had sheltered during the night.

We couldn't believe it — the factory where we had taken shelter had had a direct hit and it was all in the river. I couldn't help feeling very sad about the night watchman.

On December 12, 1940, J. Goodwin went to the Empire Theatre four miles outside Sheffield. Henry Hall and his dance band were making an appearance there:

WE HAD HARDLY SETTLED into our seats when an announcement heralded the news of an air-raid alert. Not long after, Henry Hall asked us to leave, as events were getting hectic. On reaching the street by the back entrance, we could see the windows of shops already reflecting fires burning. The scream of falling bombs put us to flight.

Off we raced hell for leather, coming to a ramp down to a garage under a building. Then like two jack rabbits, we went down our bolt hole at breakneck speed, scattering people looking out.

Peering out during a lull, I saw a face outlined against filtering plumes of smoke. Hardly had I voiced my opinion — the place was on fire — when an air-raid warden appeared. "First 10 follow me," he said. As the group retreated before our eyes, the anti-aircraft guns around the city opened up. The warden's protégés ran amok in total panic amid screams of terror. He returned empty-handed, my friend and I volunteered to follow, but I do not remember many participants.

The guns had ceased by the time we reached the designated shelter through some double doors off the street. We climbed up wooden steps to the top tier of a double-decker shelter.

I found a cubicle holding a sparkling new toilet and parked myself on the seat, much to my friend's amusement. In a hushed atmosphere the toilet gave a loud clank as I moved position, which caused the occupants to duck and cover their faces. Not because of the hun, but that damn fellow on the loo.

There were long line-ups for Charlie Chaplin and *The Great Dictator* at the Gaumont in the Haymarket, and just across the square at the Empire, Judy Garland and Mickey Rooney were strutting their stuff in *Strike up the Band*. For those who needed a good cry, *All This and Heaven Too*, with Bette Davis and Charles Boyer, was at the Warner cinema.

For those who wanted live shows there were 12 in the West End. The most famous of these was the show at the Windmill.

Since adopting the slogan We Never Close, it had attracted large numbers of servicemen who were on leave and in need of a relaxing hour spent watching scantily dressed dancing girls.

The Luftwaffe still refused to be daunted in their efforts to burn London to the ground. More than 3000 incendiary bombs were dropped on December 8, and again the emergency defence services scrambled to tackle the many fires. The nightly attacks continued till Christmas. For many it was a lonely time. Loved ones were either far away or else killed or maimed in a war that most had thought would have been long over.

Betty Westwell had arrived back home in Salford, Lancashire, just before Christmas:

I HAD BEEN going to stay with Elsie (a friend) overnight but cancelled this as my brother was arriving home. This was to be the night it was "our turn," and we were ensconced in our Anderson shelter as the bombers arrived. Elsie's house was hit, and sadly, she died. After the all-clear sounded we were amazed to see that the blast had blown out all the windows and killed our budgie in his cage.

My brother was worried because he had not bought his Christmas presents — no one realized the extent of the bombing and, though it seems incredible looking back now, my brother and I walked to Manchester. We were in awe at the damage.

Market Street was roped off and the firemen were still busy with hoses putting out fires. We thought this was quite exciting and were unaware of any danger. Shop windows were smashed and the contents were spewed onto the Market Street pavements. We were directed away from the main streets and eventually arrived at our destination — Lewis's — and were not at all surprised that the store was open. The Christmas decorations and trees were there, so everything seemed all right.

When we arrived home, my father, who was a resourceful man, had taken up the "lino" from the bedroom floors, made frames and covered the windows, creating total blackout.

The next night saw us again in the shelter, and this time things seemed worse. We lived near the railway and Salford Docks, so a direct hit was not improbable. We seemed to be in that shelter for hours, and during a quiet spell, my father dashed out to the house to fill the kettle. He flew back into the shelter with a look of disbelief on his face. Then there was the loudest explosion I have ever heard, then uncanny silence. Afterward we discovered that what my father had seen, sailing over our house, was a land mine — which had scored a direct hit on the street behind ours. Homes and lives were lost.

When we finally went back into the house we discovered that the blast had blown out all the lino and my father said some very cryptic things about Hitler.

We had no gas, electricity or water — but we had each other and our house was intact. People who had lost their homes were streaming along the streets to be accommodated in church halls. I thought everyone was leaving except us.

My father was a member of the Home Guard and reported for duty to see what he could do to help. It turned out that the cemetery had been hit.

He didn't tell us for a long time afterward that they were collecting the scattered bones.

What a joy when he returned. He had been given a Christmas hamper containing large tins of chicken and ham and fruits and Christmas pudding. The lino was tacked back on the frames and so eliminated the draught from the open windows. We ate our Christmas dinner by candlelight and gave out our presents. It was the most unusual Christmas I can ever remember.

King George decided to deliver the traditional Christmas message to his subjects. Because he had a slight speech impediment, public speaking was not something he was fond of doing; but this time, the nation's first Christmas of the war, he felt compelled to let everyone know, especially the troops at home and abroad, that he, too, felt their suffering and was with them in spirit at the front line.

His Christmas greeting of 1940 had a special magic, as his stammer gave it a sincere human quality. And he stirred everyone to greater effort as he talked of "being in the front line together."

"Lovely," said Nell.
"Bloody marvellous," said Alf.

12

FIRE
OVER
LONDON

IF ONE BOMB in the garden of Buckingham Palace had given the King an idea of how it felt to be at the front line, the raid of December 29, 1940, would intensify the feeling.

On the night of December 20, the RAF had pounded Berlin for several hours, reducing freight yards, railway stations and homes to rubble. Hitler had turned to Goering, who had once promised that no enemy aircraft would ever cross the fatherland, and screamed, "Retaliate, retaliate, retaliate!"

In the Paris headquarters of Field Marshal Hugo Sperrle, the general in command of Luftflotte-Three, heads were bent low over a large map of England spread before them. The word had arrived from the fuehrer: London was to be hit as never before.

Hugo Sperrle was the Hollywood version of the perfect Teutonic villain, complete with a monocle and short-cropped hair. The general had been leading the raids on London since September, and although he had not been able to force Churchill to negotiate a peace, the damage had been satisfying. A week earlier, a raid on Manchester, in which thousands of fire bombs had blanketed the city, had reduced whole areas to smouldering ruins. Why not direct the same kind of attack on London?

All agreed that the next raid would concentrate on the use of incendiary bombs, but it needed careful planning. First the weather had to be right. For more than a week, fog and overcast skies had restricted flying from the French airfields. The latest reports claimed that this weather was lifting, although there was talk of an approaching storm front.

They chose December 29 as the ideal date. The position of the moon would mean particularly low tides in the upper reaches of the Thames. Since this was where the London fire services looked for their water supplies, the timing of the fire raid was ideal.

December 29 was also a Sunday. The business section of London would be closed and most working people would be at home or in the country. Roof spotters would still be enjoying the Christmas week and few would feel like spending time on the roofs of their offices. By the time the fire watchers and roof observers had got to their posts the damage would have been done.

Hitler listened to the various arguments for and against a massive fire raid on London on that date and gave his opinion to Goering, who passed the word down the line to Hugo Sperrle anxiously waiting in the Hotel Luxembourg in Paris. The raid was on.

The first planes over the target area would set the initial fires, lighting a path for those coming behind. One squadron of 20 bombers would be led by the much decorated Hauptmann Friedrich Aschenbrenner, who was the obvious choice for the job. The veteran of dozens of bombing missions, he had persuaded the authorities to give him only the best and most experienced of pilots and crew. They quickly built a reputation throughout the German air force and were given the nickname the Fire Raisers.

As the planes left the southern tip of Brittany and climbed toward the British coast, Aschenbrenner thought how much easier it was to find the target than it had been in the earlier days. Now they had the X-apparatus, an almost foolproof electronic aid to navigation. The radio receiver in the aircraft picked up a primary radio beam sent from the peninsula. All they had to do was fly along the beam until they reached the target. Aschenbrenner glanced at his instrument panel. Altitude: 6000 feet. Speed: 180 mph. He should be over the city of London at 6:08 P.M. He was.

As London's firefighters leapt to their engines, they knew that this was going to be a night like no other. The first bombs had fallen in Southwark, close to one of the main fire stations, and as they clanged their way through the streets surrounding London Bridge, the whole sky was alive with falling incendiary bombs.

Some bounced and spat their flames along the pavements, but most buried themselves deep in the timbers of the south bank and its warehouses. Within minutes flames were leaping from one to the other like a giant forest fire.

Although St. Paul's Cathedral was still unscathed, the streets surrounding Sir Christopher Wren's masterpiece were charred rubble on which more and more buildings seemed to collapse.

Banks, offices, churches and houses were ablaze, and as the firefighters attempted to direct their hoses to what they judged the most dangerous of the fires, the main water supply in the area was hit. Suddenly only a trickle of water came from the hoses. The firemen headed for the Thames and waded through the mud of an exceptionally low tide in an attempt to get to the only water available. The area around St. Paul's soon became a roaring inferno.

Jean Dumpleton was a 20-year-old telephonist who lived in Upper Norwood, London:

LOOKING BACK, I think December 29, 1940, was our worst experience. We all thought our beloved city would surely be completely devastated. It was a very dark night, and I had just left the station. Then the sirens sounded. I ran into my local news agent's for some cigarettes (hoping they could let me have 10), had a little chat and when I came out of the shop I couldn't believe my eyes. I had never seen so many flares coming down from the skies before or since. It looked like a fairyland.

I was fascinated, I was alone, for everyone had beaten it home. I watched for a few seconds, realized that there were enemy aircraft overhead, realized my danger and ran hell for leather home.

I thought we were in for a rough ride that night. I made a flask of tea for the shelter as usual, and made my way down the back stairs.

Neighbours had gathered in various shelters and I could hear them talking. Being of a nosy nature, wondering whether all was in order for the night vigil, I went to inquire. They were talking about London being on fire. "If you go to the top of the hill you can see the city is ablaze." Well, although enemy aircraft were about, it wasn't too bad in our district at the time, so a few of us decided to go and see what all the commotion was about.

I have never forgotten that blazing sky. It was uncanny. It was all so red and vicious, and you could see flames and smoke rising clearly into the darkness of the night. There were a lot of people at the top of the hill that night, but not for long. We heard high explosives being dropped, the vibration increased, and then it seemed as though all hell had been let loose. We made a hasty retreat back to our shelters.

It was the most frightening night I can recall. My cat's eyes were like two yellow pools, large and bright. He no longer slept but literally leapt up toward my face suddenly, his tail swishing as he did so. He was scared and no mistake. The night-lights flickered, making patterns on the wavy ridges of the shelter walls. Bombs were raining down fast and furious now, and you could hear the anti-aircraft guns firing at top speed, not far away. The noise was terrific. I was as scared as my cat. The shelter vibrated several times and I had visions of being buried.

When the raid eventually eased off, I cannot remember whether I slept. I had tea from the flask. I could have done with a double brandy. My cat slept peacefully.

I cannot remember the time the all-clear sounded, but we struggled out of our shelters in our siren suits, washed, cleaned our teeth, made some coffee and toast to begin the new day. Everyone was talking about the raid on the station platform as we waited for the train. It was late. We all wondered whether we would be able to get to the city and we all felt shattered. I had noticed a few buildings which had "caught it" on Anerley Hill. Shop fronts had disappeared, windows were shattered and broken fragments of glass were everywhere.

The ARP men were out in force trying their best to cope with everything.

Our train duly arrived. I wondered if the building where I worked would still be there, as I knew full well that we had really caught a packet that night. I dozed off in the train and so didn't notice any bomb damage on the journey.

When the train arrived at London Bridge, I shot down the tube to the Bank station, and when I came up to the Cornhill exit there was a horrid smell of smoke. Hoses were everywhere, it was very wet and some of the exhausted firemen were being supplied with tea by the WVS and early-morning office cleaners.

It was pretty chaotic one way and another. I could see the main buildings were still intact — Royal Exchange, Manor House, Bank of England. The building where I worked was undamaged.

The brave firemen had come from districts in and around London to fight the inferno. So many lost their lives that night. Without their heroism in dealing with the appalling situation I dread to think what the outcome would have been.

Life carried on through the winter months, and we managed to get to work somehow, undaunted and not to be beaten. A milkman gave me a lift one morning on his horse-driven cart as far as the Elephant and Castle. Hilarious really, properly dressed for the city in a smart hat, gloves (in those days), a nice dress and very high-heeled court shoes. Well, we had to keep the flag flying, didn't we?

Evenings during the winter months were one dash home from the office, trying to make it before the siren sounded. We had a very nice friendly pub near to where I lived called the Rising Sun. It was kept by a middle-aged couple, and to break the monotony of sitting in the Anderson shelter trying to read by night-light, we would spend part of some evenings in there. I well remember a gin-and-lime at eight pence a glass.

If the "flake" got heavy (there were mobile gun batteries outside) and Jerry got rather too tiresome, the pub landlord would allow us to go down the cellar. Then we let rip with a singsong.

I had a nasty piece of shrapnel come through my kitchen one evening when I had decided to try to make a proper meal; it came through the door at such speed and buried itself in the wall opposite. I had only just got up from the table to look at my rice pudding in the oven. The whizzing sound was terrific, and in fright I dropped the almost cooked rice pudding onto the matting, which took days to remove with a fork!

Mr. A. Martin was a trained voluntary air-raid warden. He also did shift work as a stoker for a block of residential flats. He was on duty as the night-shift stoker at the Mansion Flats in Bloomsbury on the night of December 29:

MY FIRST INKLING of the extent of the raid was when I noticed that all the water gauges in the boiler houses were dropping fast and I had to move like hell to empty the fire boxes.

The bombing was so heavy that most of the water mains burst and the fires so fierce that the firemen had to draw water from the Thames.

With one of the house porters I stood on the roof and watched the city burn. It was necessary to be up there because fire bombs were dropping everywhere. It was an awesome sight. Away to our right a sea of fire stretched from Trafalgar Square right along to St. Paul's. As a stiffening breeze cleared some of the smoke, the dome of the great cathedral was silhouetted against the flames. The swish of water from many hoses could be plainly heard, and also the cries of the human beings who were somewhere at work in that inferno.

Now and then there was a surge of bright light to the sky as another missile found its target. Away to our left the university library was in flames and pieces of charred manuscript drifted onto our roof. When my relief came at eight the next morning, although I was dog-tired, I ventured into the city as far as possible. It was amazing to see the city gents, wearing bowlers and carrying umbrellas and briefcases, trying to get to their offices as though nothing had happened.

John Davey was standing on the porch with his dad, an old neighbour they called Mister, and his dog:

MR. CICANOWITZ, who was Dutch, was known as Mister simply because we could not pronounce his name. It was still night when suddenly we heard the drone of a plane which dropped several flares like a giant fireworks display.

The next thing I knew, everything went grey and I was falling. I eventually settled on my side, trapped by the rubble of our demolished house. I was screaming abuse. My dad's voice came from somewhere near and said, "Don't worry, son. They'll get you out." Mister just called my dad's name a few times.

After a while I heard voices up above; they heard my shouts and the rescue operations began. From then on I could see the stars in the sky through a small gap.

I could hear the dog trying to find his way out, and I shouted up to the rescue workers for them to watch where he came out, which they did, and this gave them an idea where I was. I eventually asked them to lower a torch, which they did, and I guided them to me.

The marvellous rescue workers toiled throughout the night, and I was finally rescued after eight hours, but unfortunately my dad, age 41, and Mister did not survive.

Wyn Wheatcroft had taken the train from Epping to London to meet her three brothers, who were on their way home from being evacuated:

THEY DIDN'T TURN UP for the second time, so I made my way back to Liverpool Street station. I was only 14 at the time and when I went to the station to get on the train a policeman there asked, "Where are you going, missy?" I told him I was going to Epping. "Not tonight, you're not," he replied. "The line has been bombed at Leyton."

He told me to go to Maryland station where a policeman would take me to a shelter. The shelter was over the toilets on an island in the road. It was filled with people as it was the night they were to bomb London with thousands of incendiary bombs.

There were lots of bus drivers who kept coming in saying it was like bonfire night out there. I was being made a fuss of by the bus drivers. They were buying me buns and cups of tea. I don't think I realized how bad it was outside. I remember a WAAF was very kind to me and saw me home the next day.

I got a real good hiding when I got home from my mum as she had been worrying about me all night.

W. A. Rice was a leading fireman in London and had been called to a house that was completely destroyed. The mother, father and daughter were in an Anderson shelter and had been rescued. Unfortunately another daughter was in a cot still inside:

FALLEN TIMBERS made it impossible to free her from above. Most wardens were fairly hefty fellows and unable to get through the small entrance. One fellow, who was slightly built, was getting through when I arrived, so I decided to go, too, and give him assistance. We found that it was impossible to get her from the cot, owing to the number of timbers lying across it, and decided she would have to be freed from the bottom.

We acquired some cutters and slowly cut away the base and freed her, but our worry was what might shift. We finally got her free and with her parents again.

I looked for my vehicle and found that it had been directed back to the station. When I got back to Brixton station, I was immediately put on charge for neglecting my duty and threatened that I might lose my position as a leading fireman. This annoyed me, and I told them that I would rather be just a fireman in case something of this nature happened again, and after some discussion my explanation was accepted.

E. V. Thompson was a member of the Auxiliary Fire Service in London:

MY DUTY was to drive a Ford V8 with a Denis Pump Trailer. About 10 o'clock that night our crew had a call to report to Stratford Broadway. We immediately started out driving in the pitch dark, very little light as our headlamps were masked, allowing only slits of light. As we neared London the sky was lit up with flares and the glow of already started fires.

Arriving at the Stratford Fire Station, we were instructed to proceed to Bromley Gas Works, as various fires were raging there. We were now in the thick of the raid, and mines, bombs and incendiaries were falling as if all hell had been let loose. Under those conditions we had little idea as to the route we should take. Another fire crew knew the way and told us to drive close on their tail.

Keeping very close behind, we were progressing along the Plaistow Road when there was a crash, as another cascade of incendiaries dropped on the road and houses. With the light from the fires I could plainly see the pump in front.

It was then I had a strange feeling as if a voice was saying, "Disobey orders and let the leading truck draw away." As I lifted my foot from the accelerator, dropping behind, I heard shouts. Suddenly I felt as if I was being carried away in a blast of hot sand, and noise got louder and louder, then I blacked out. I regained consciousness quickly, and my immediate thought was that I was trapped in a burning vehicle. Crawling out of the car, I knelt on the ground. Debris was falling, but my senses told me that although I could not use my steel helmet (it had blown away) I must protect my head. Crawling back to the van, I felt the door opening and lay with my head and shoulders inside until picked up by an air-raid warden who took me to his post and gave me first aid until an ambulance arrived.

Then two wardens came in, most distressed, having to inform the warden attending me that his house had been completely destroyed, and there was little hope for his family getting out alive.

A terrible amount of damage had been caused by a parachute mine that had dropped beside the pump I'd been following. The pump crew were all killed, and debris had blasted into my car.

The ambulance arrived, and it was driven by a young woman. On the way to the hospital she stopped to pick up a woman on the road. This woman was swearing like a trooper and vowing she had only come to the front gate to find out what all the commotion was. A brick must have dropped on her head, knocking her unconscious. She was now partially recovered, bleeding badly, and her outcry was that her husband indoors would not know where she had gone. We arrived at hospital to find that it, too, had been bombed.

Conditions were not good. Water supplies were short. There seemed no room for the wounded. The hospital staff were coping to the best of their ability. Many patients were kept on the floor in a large hall. During the night the doctors and nurses treated our wounds. I was black from head to foot from the explosive, unable to bathe owing to the lack of water.

John Hadley was with the London Fire Brigade:

DURING ONE RAID a scruffy mongrel terrier wandered into our station in Lillie Road school. We adopted him and called him Red. He remained with us until we were closed by enemy action, when he was transferred, with some of the personnel, to the station at Fulham Road.

Red was a bit of a nuisance. When the bells went off for a fire, he would go running along beside the appliances until he was out of breath. He remained at the local station until after the war and was taken on a fire appliance for his final journey.

As Londoners made their way to work the following Monday morning and emerged from the underground, they looked in horror at what was left of this centre of British commerce. Most spent the following days attempting to clear up the mess in their office buildings. Many found they had no office building at all, just a mountain of bricks and smouldering ashes.

For Nell the daylight brought dreadful news. Her long-time friend and neighbour, Irene Thurbin, and her daughter, Patty, had both been killed. They had recently moved to a flat that offered much better living conditions than those at St. George's Buildings, and their new residence had received a direct hit.

The visit from German bombers that began December 29 lasted 48 hours. The problems they left in their wake were many. The water supply for firefighters had been virtually cut off. Their equipment left much to be desired. And the shelters that had seen their share of damage needed assistance. The Bank tube station, which so many Londoners had entered for safety, had received a direct hit and 111 had been killed. It seemed the people of Britain had nowhere to hide.

Fortunately the raids on London began to ease up in the new year, allowing the authorities time to deal with the various problems. The fire service was given new equipment. New water mains were laid to ensure that never again would firemen have to suck their way through the mud of the Thames in search of water.

As the new year of 1941 began everyone wondered what the future held. Many had come to the end of their tethers.

Nell told Alf in no uncertain terms that she for one was right fed up with spending her time underground with buckets for toilets. It was okay for Churchill and the other toffs to declare they could take it. "So could I," said Nell, "if I lived in bleedin' Downing Street with its comfortable shelter, or could put me feet up in Buckingham Palace and Windsor Castle."

"If it's as bad as you say down there," said Alf, who had yet to go down for cover, "then why don't yer join the Communist party and march with them?"

"What time 'ave I got to march wiv anyone? Time I gets ta work and back for washing and get your food on the table I'm lucky if I 'as time to put me shoes on, let alone march."

Thousands did have time to put their shoes on and were soon seen in central London calling for a "people's peace."

Ivy Griffiths remembers resisting someone's attempt to persuade her to join a march on London:

AFTER NIGHT after night of bombings, the planes came over early without warning, and I was making a mad dash to the shelter at Grandma's when Mrs. Greaves, my next-door neighbour, came dashing after me and, grabbing my arm, said, "Come with me. I've had enough and am going to march to London here and now and put an end to the bombing."

Suddenly there was an almighty bang. She turned tail and ran and I made for the shelter as fast as I could. That was the end of any further suggestions of a march to London.

Fortunately for the British, dreadful weather forced the Luftwaffe to stay put for a month, and the population of London experienced a period of quiet through February. An uneasy government took the time to tackle the problems that had forced so many into the streets in protest.

Thousands of bunk beds began to appear in the large shelters, which helped to smother the growing discontent.

When Alf got home from work, Nell had some sad news for him: Milk Bottle Annie had passed away. This much beloved "lady of the evening" would no longer be seen. Her strange nickname had come about because of her habit of placing an empty milk bottle on the windowsill of her flat to tell whoever was interested in her favours that she was occupied with a customer.

In a time of many deaths, hers stood out. Annie's long-time companion, Albert Nooks, was questioned by the police for many hours. It seems that poor Annie had been dead for three days before Albert reported the fact. Albert told the coroner that he finally went to his neighbour, Eddy Thompson, and said, "I fink there's somefink wrong wiv Annie. She ain't drunk 'er tea." He claimed that he had been unaware of her passing until he noted that she had six cups of tea beside her. All untouched.

It was not surprising that the police were not completely satisfied with his story.

Milk Bottle Annie had had a heart of gold, and as Nell said, "Never did anyone any 'arm. Anyone down on their luck could go to Annie. They could even sleep between her and Albert if they didn't have a bed." And many did.

Alf Smith, the undertaker, gave her a wonderful send-off. During the funeral procession everyone made sure that they were staring at the ground as Alf Smith passed, because if he nodded toward you, then you would be the next one to be carried out "toes up." With the number of people killed in the blitz this was no time to take chances.

13

THE
CIVILIANS
SOLDIER ON

TOM DUNNE was 11 years old and living in Manchester with his parents. During a particularly heavy raid in December, his oldest brother, Gerard, was out and unable to get home. His father had refused the government's offer of a shelter, believing that it was impossible for the Germans to bomb the area where they lived:

IN THE HOUSE was my older brother, Eddie, age 13, my younger brother, Paul, age six, and Leo, the baby, age 18 months, who was asleep in his cot in the back bedroom. I remember a neighbour calling and begging my dad to share his air-raid shelter. Dad refused. Later, Paul and I went to bed in the same room as Leo, but sleeping in a double bed. The blitz continued, but like most children we soon fell asleep. My next memory was waking up and I was floating upward — it seemed in slow motion. The roof was opening up and I was flying toward the stars. No pain, no special sensation, the oblivion — a parachute mine had done its job.

How long I was unconscious is open to conjecture, but it must have been several hours. When I woke up I was choking with brick dust, and I was cold and very dazed; I was buried in my bed. I could see that the roof had gone and that there was no rear wall to the house or any dividing walls. Looking to my right, I could see that Leo's cot was no longer there, just a pile of rubble. One thing that really imprinted itself in my mind was a large statue of Our Lady standing upright in a corner of the bedroom.

I realized that I must get myself up to dig for Leo and was clearing debris off myself, when Paul, who up to this point I had not thought about, started moving under rubble near me. I was free and started digging. Luckily he was not buried deeply and seemed unhurt. When I uncovered him he became hysterical and I remember slapping his face to stop him — which he did. He lay quietly and I told him I must try to find baby Leo. I started digging with bare hands near to the corner, lifting rubble and placing it in the region of my bed. I kept finding pieces of the cot, no bigger than a cigarette package, and I really felt I was not going to find my baby brother. Suddenly I heard a whimper. I speeded up the digging and there he was. All his night clothes were missing and he was naked and jet black. I cleared his mouth and eyes and lifted him up into my arms. Apparently none the worse, he cried loudly. It was a wonderful sound. Then and only then did I think of shouting for help, which I did very loudly. Paul joined in.

Our shouts really startled the rescuers outside in Platt Lane. They had just kept a watch on the devastation — waiting for daylight to dig our bodies out. We had apparently been unconscious for so long that the emergency-rescue services had removed my mother's body from the downstairs living room (she'd been killed instantly) and my father, who was only dazed. Unfortunately my father had wandered off in his shocked state and sustained major head injuries (not fatal) from anti-aircraft shrapnel, which was falling like rain. They had searched for us and had obviously concluded that we were dead.

At the police station we were made comfortable with blankets and cocoa. Outside, the blitz raged on unabated. I was still dazed. Suddenly a bomb landed near the police station and shook the building. Sometime later a policeman came in, screaming that his wife and children had just been killed. A police sergeant tried to pacify him and nodded toward us lying there and said, "Calm down. You're not the only one with trouble."

Sonia Walker was allowed to go to the entrance of her shelter near Liverpool and watch the bombers overhead. She does not remember being frightened, only excited:

MY MOTHER would play and encourage us to sing around the piano as a family. One day when I must have been about five, my mother asked me to choose a song — I asked her for the air-raid shelter hymn. She eventually found out that I meant — "Oh, God, our help in ages past...our shelter from the stormy blast..."

Alf Wicks wasn't the only one who learned how to recognize the different planes. Although only 12, James Giles considered himself an expert:

MY FRIEND PETER was 11. We stood chatting outside my home when an airplane appeared overhead. "Wow, that's a German Junkers 90," I said. "No," said Peter. "There's no air raid on — it's an RAF Blenheim." "Bet you it's a Junkers," I replied. Suddenly we saw clearly a bomb descending from its underbelly. We shot into the house; a loud explosion followed. "Told you so!" I muttered.

Pauline Scowen was 11. She had been evacuated but returned in 1940 to her home in London:

WE LIVED on an estate in Wandsworth and some of the ground-floor flats were made into air-raid shelters by means of iron poles fitted in to strengthen them. However, when the top block of flats was hit one night (we lived on a hill and the block we lived in was at the bottom) all the people in the shelters were crushed because the iron poles buckled.

They changed these to wooden beams after that, but my mother had lost faith in the shelters by then, so we stayed in our own flat. I remember her saying, "If we go, we all go together."

I remember at school being told to be very quiet in the playground, because the firefighters had been fighting fires all night and were trying to sleep. We stood around in little groups whispering and sometimes watching the dogfights high in the sky. The boys always knew which were ours.

The railway line ran at the back of us, and at night, a train, fitted with what was called a pom-pom gun, would go past, firing at the bombers lit up by the searchlights.

I started work at Ross Optical works in Clapham Common, and often one of the women — for it was mostly women doing the war work — would not come to work one morning and we would later hear that her house had been bombed that night and we would not see her again. There would then be a collection for a wreath.

Geoffrey Clappison and his parents had been living with friends until it was safe for them to return to their home in Hull:

205

WHEN WE RETURNED home there was some damage to the house, with windows smashed. Amazingly enough our pet budgie was still alive and chirping, despite the fact his cage had been blown to the floor and deposited under the table.

Mary Chamberlain (now Constance) was 16. Her father owned a cinema in Bristol, and although the sirens wailed often enough, her family had yet to construct a shelter:

THIS WAS TO BE the wood shed and coal cellar which faced you as you came down a flight of concrete steps from the kitchen into the large reinforced cellar that formed the foundation of our house. But for the time being we were to use a room under the main stairs in the cinema.

At first we thought it was fun. If the sirens went off in the daytime (invariably at mealtimes) we would all march out, complete with plates of food, round the back of the house which with two shops and the cinema formed a block of buildings. We would go in through the back door and up the outside steps which led to the operating room, and eventually into this little room under the stairs. If the raid was likely to come that night we would don siren suits. My sister always seemed very brave and well organized (she made sure the hangers in the wardrobe all faced the same way to enable us to remove the clothes quickly — a practice I maintain to this day!).

I, however, was scared stiff, especially when I first realized that this nightly ritual might go on for a long time.

The fun soon wore off. Bunk beds were installed in the cinema shelter. We often awoke in the night, and our mother would give us tea and biscuits, then we'd settle down for what we hoped would be a peaceful night. It was my mother who first noticed what was happening, and it must have been her exclamation that woke us up. In the glow of the nightlight we watched as a family of mice scuttled around the legs of our bunks, enjoying the feast of biscuit crumbs we had dropped.

"That does it!" said my mother. "Hitler can come and bomb us at home. This is positively the last night I spend in here!"

The cinema shelter had no windows, of course, but there was a ventilation shaft. Should the cinema collapse around us it would be possible to crawl through this and out through an opening in the outside wall onto the stairs leading from the operating box. When my mother realized where the mice were coming from she made a firm stand. Neither Hitler nor anyone else was going to make her crawl though that shaft past a row of dust-encrusted pipes and generations of mice.

I do not remember exactly when we moved into our finally completed cellar shelter. I think it must have been the first time we had a real raid. Father had fixed up a very tiny emergency electric light. The first stick bombs fell, cut off the power and blew away the small curtain that covered the one small window. Father decided that he had better not switch on his light. Through the window we could see a great red glow.

"Good God, Roy!" exclaimed Mother. "D'you really think with all that hell going on out there they're goin' to see that miserable bulb? Switch it on!" But for some reason it wouldn't work then, and it never did.

With their steeples standing out like beacons, the local churches attracted many of the bombs. Alex Crawford was an apprentice joiner during the Glasgow and Clydebank blitz in March 1941. He found himself running back and forth with timber shoring up buildings to assist rescue crews:

ON THIS PARTICULAR OCCASION I travelled from our work place in Goven to Clydebank, a distance of about four miles, to Kilbowie Road. I was horrified at the sight which met me. There was hardly a building left standing, but in the midst of all this chaos was Radnor Park Church, and it was another joiner's and my job to shore up the pillars from the balcony to the roof, which had been knocked off plumb with the blast, and there was a danger of the roof falling in.

We did manage to shore up each pillar, plumb it and then lower it back in place.

The main thing that struck me was that there were hundreds of incendiary bombs lying in the seats. Two were even on a soft seat in the minister's vestry, but it was the only building in the whole area that did not burn.

Eileen Paterson was the youngest of four and was with her mother and a sister in the wash house at the back of her Clydebank home when an explosion blew in the windows.

MUM LAY OVER ME and my sister to protect us. Later the house caught fire, and I remember being carried in a blanket along the street. I also remember —

Everything on fire. All the windows of tenement buildings nearby alight. John Brown's Wood Yard blazing. Dad and brother passing each other on the stairs when blown in opposite directions. Brother out in Montrose Street giving stray cats milk as bombs fell. Mum cross when incendiary bomb landed on wardrobe, which was put out with precious sack of flour and warm water from someone's greenhouse. (Flour and paste everywhere!). Two goats found sitting in armchairs when man searching houses for survivors. Food lorry coming to deliver sandwiches — Mum keeping this food till correct mealtime.

In the face of the horrific there is always humour. G. Davies lived in Liverpool, close to the docks, and had come through a fierce weekend bombing:

ON THE MONDAY I went to the Co-Op grocers and was shocked to see the front blown away. A customer commented,

"How awful!" And with typical Liverpool wit an assistant said, "You should see our Berlin branch."

Diana Jones (now Palmer) was 12 and living with her family in Liverpool. Her parents had a confirmed shelter space for the whole family under the fish market in the city centre.

WE HAD LEFT mattresses and bedding down there. It was a horrible place, and my older sister and I used to go to the Capital cinema when we could, even though the sirens had started, to delay the moment of going to bed in the shelter. We would walk through the blackout into town, watching bombs fall and searchlights and the mobile artillery firing at the enemy. Looking back, we were either totally stupid or fearless. Anything to delay that horrible shelter.

The stench in it was fearsome. It was packed with children, mothers, old men. There must have been some way for us to obtain hot water for tea, for we always had a hot drink.

We had grown used to the bombing, shrapnel, et cetera, but this one night stands out in my memory.

The alert had sounded, and so we were under the fish market. We were all tired, night after night of bombing, and sleep was hard to come by — too much talking and air-raid wardens coming and telling everyone of thousands of bombers overhead. Liverpool burning.

Then there was a great uproar. My dad grabbed my next-to-youngest sister, who for some reason had huge swollen legs, my mum carried the youngest one, and we were being led up many stairs. On the way we had to walk through gas escaping from the refrigerators. The stairs seemed to go on and on and in a circular way. When we came out, the air was thick with smoke, and everywhere was burning. One of my sisters was sick and dizzy with the gas, we had been sleeping on the wet ground, and firemen were black and exhausted.

My dad, my frail old dad, somehow managed to keep carrying my sick sister and keep us together. There was panic, lots and lots of airplanes, the sky red, people running and searching for shelter, bombs and fire bombs exploding all over. My mum and dad led us across the road to where the old Forum cinema was burning. We ran under the ladders of the firefighters with flames and smoke and debris all around. Some splinters hit me. Everywhere people were running this way and that, searching for shelter.

My dad spotted an open doorway opposite Blackler's, also well ablaze, with two air-raid wardens looking up at the sky. He got us across the road, and the warden said that there was no room, but my dad begged him to let us in for the children's sake. He said, "Hurry up, I'll have to close the door. They're packed like sardines down there."

This shelter was under a butcher shop, where St. John's market now stands. It was so full there was no room to sit. The smell from the overflowing buckets used for toilet purposes was something I'll remember always. We all leaned on each other. People were banging on the door upstairs begging to be let in. It was impossible. Many people wandered around outside searching and died that night.

Toward dawn, my older sister and I could stand the smell of the place no longer and told my dad we were going home. He let us go.

We came out to a beautiful red sky and smoke and flames, also an unexploded bomb lying at the side of the shelter we were in. Its nose was buried in the concrete and soldiers surrounded it.

It was an amazing sight. My sister and I just wandered around for a bit, glad to be able to move, looking at all the shops on fire or just burned out and smouldering. There were men digging in the rubble, searching for people and dragging out bodies. We reached Lewis's, just a shell now, and made our way home up Brownlow Hill.

We saw lorries piled with dead people being covered with tarpaulins, and when the lorries moved, the bodies wobbled under the tarpaulins.

We met our brother in his naval uniform. His face and uniform were black, his eyes so tired and hurt looking. He had been on leave and had left his newborn daughter and wife to help with rescue work. He pushed his cap up and was nearly crying. I heard the helpless anger in his voice when he told how he'd dug half-burned dead women and children out of the ruins. He said at least we, meaning the forces, can fight back.

That was the last time we saw our brother. He sailed a few days later and was reported missing in action.

Louis Day was 15 and living in Liverpool. He had just received his first bike and was planning a trip with his friend to Chester. When a heavy raid was carried out on the city on the Saturday it looked as though his Sunday outing would be postponed:

AS THE BOMBS were getting increasingly closer, Mum got us up from bed and we huddled in the corner of our small brick shelter. There was Mum, my sister, Sylvia, age 10, and me. Dad was on fire-watching duty that night and so was outside on the streets keeping a look-out with a companion for incendiary bombs. He popped back every now and again to see that we were all right.

About 10 minutes after he had been in to see us on the last occasion, the bombing, bangs and thuds got closer and closer until there was the most almighty crash and all the lights went out. Brick dust filled the air, and we couldn't see a thing. After a minute or so Mum produced a flashlamp and we could see that our little shelter was the only thing still standing. The cellar had collapsed completely, obliterating the beds. Broken beams were down to the floor and rubble was everywhere.

Sometime later we heard a faint voice calling. We thought it was Dad, but it was in fact a police search party looking for survivors.

We all three shouted, "Help! Help!" as loud as we could and we were very relieved when our cries were answered. The faint sound of digging could be heard, and after a while a small hole was forced through in the vicinity of the grating above our heads. A small stirrup-pump hose was fed down to us and I sprayed the water on the fast-approaching flames. About 15 minutes later the rescuers made a hole big enough for us to be pulled out of the shelter one at a time. When we got out we were amazed to see that we were on the edge of a tremendous crater which was a mass of flames. We were taken by ambulance to Bootle Hospital, and quite miraculously not one of us had a scratch.

We found out shortly afterward that the crater had been caused by two parachuted land mines that had tangled together, and our father was caught in the blast and killed instantly.

I returned to the crater a week or two later. It was still smouldering slightly and there at the very bottom was what remained of my new bike. A twisted heap of tubes. I borrowed some tools and removed the three-speed gears for future use. This and my dad's broken pipe were all we salvaged.

Jean McWilliam was 12 when the Germans turned their attention to Merseyside. Her father, a headmaster, was exempt from call-up for the forces, but had joined the ARP. Along with her mother and grandmother she lived in a house that was well protected from the bombing.

OUR HOUSE, like many others, had the lower windows at the back completely sandbagged as protection against bomb blast, and my grandmother and I slept in the downstairs dining room against the inner walls.

In the event of an air raid during the night — a frequent occurrence — my grandmother and I, as the oldest and youngest members of the household, would be hustled down to a neighbour's house where they had an indoor shelter. This was located in a downstairs room and was known as the "battleship" shelter. We sat in this protected area in comparative comfort with a couple of old dears from the neighbourhood, drinking tea, eating biscuits, knitting, sewing and generally discussing the destruction being wrought all around us.

During these sojourns in the shelter it was customary for my mother, in deference to my grandmother's wishes, to wear on her head an old handle-less saucepan stuffed with a scarf. As a measure of protection against shrapnel it was worse than useless, but it pleased and reassured the old lady. It was also a source of comic amusement, the anxious face beneath the adornment emphasizing the absurdity of the device, but it helped morale no end. The toddler next door observed: "I've seen soldiers with khaki tin hats, my daddy has an air-force blue one, but I've never seen a silver one before."

Marshall Litholand and his mother lived in Liverpool, and they arrived home one day after a raid to find all the windows and the front door blown in. Two new velvet chairs were in the front room:

AS CHILDREN we were never allowed to sit on them. My mother was buying them through a club at so much per week. The chairs were ruined by soot and broken glass, and ironically she still had to pay for these for many months after they were destroyed. My mother made an effort to clean up the mess and to gather together some personal belongings. Whilst she was doing this her sister came in, very distressed. I overheard her say to my mother, "Your mother's gone."

Now, my old grandma used to visit the communal shelters during the evenings, and on this one night she went to the Durning Road College, together with hundreds more, to shelter from the bombs deep down in the cellars of the school.

On this particular night the college received a direct hit from a land mine, and the building was completely destroyed. Eight people crawled out from beneath the rubble, my grandmother being one of them. We did not know that she had survived until many days later. She evacuated herself on the day after the raid and told no one. We found out a week later when we received a letter through the post.

The parents of six-year-old Sheila McAllister decided that rather than evacuate their daughter from the Liverpool area, they would, along with her 18-month-old brother, all stick together. They had an Anderson shelter that took up most of their tiny back garden:

MY MOTHER GREW nasturtiums on it and tomatoes around the door. Sheltered by a doorway of sandbags they did very well. We also had interesting wildflowers, courtesy of the load of soil from Wales brought to cover the shelter.

Inside we were very cramped at first and it was impossible for adults to lie down. However, an extra length of corrugated iron was added, which gave us about six feet by five. We had bunks on one side for the kids and a well-chocked-up old camp bed for adults to sit on. I don't think they slept much. We had an heavy iron paraffin stove for heat, light and boiling kettles, which it did fairly well. In my siren suit, made from my father's old serge suit, I was warm, if rather itchy.

We were put to bed there at night for months. The usual inhabitants were my mother, we two children, the small baby from next door and his mother, who tended to get hysterical when things hotted up. My mother didn't. She had a carving knife on hand for the first German who showed his face!

After one raid we had no windows left anywhere in the house but the kitchen. People over the back from us called out that they had to evacuate because of an unexploded bomb. We ended up with 15 people in that one kitchen, and two dogs which hated each other. We had no water, but we had gas. My mother was cooking several minuscule weekend joints, everyone's meat hastily snatched up in the exodus. An exhausted man was asleep against the kitchen door with his tin hat over his eyes. I had never seen an adult so filthy. He, with my father, had been out on the streets all night.

When Helen Walton saw a parachute descending, she set off with several others determined to catch the enemy airman:

YOU CAN APPRECIATE that this could not be done in a straight line, but up roads and round corners, always keeping "him" in sight. Then someone realized we were chasing not a human, but a land mine gently swinging from the skies. You can imagine our immediate turnaround. This time, garden fences and any other obstacles were taken in our stride!

Margaret Hill was 11 when she and her family were pulled from their bombed house in Liverpool by rescue workers and relocated to the country. While out picking wild flowers one day, she and her sister encountered the enemy in person:

WE WALKED to the edge of the field on the farm. There were about six men working there digging trenches, which seemed to go on forever. They were speaking in a foreign language, and they wore jackets of a different sort of uniform. I'd been told that they were German POWs.

We were just about to leave when one in a naval uniform beckoned to me and in sign language asked me to bring him a cigarette the following day. I nodded to him and left. On the way home I swore my sister to secrecy. That night when my father had fallen asleep I looked up at the mantelpiece at his packet of cigarettes. I took out a cigarette very gently and put it in my blazer pocket.

The following day I raced across the field to where the Germans were working. I waited for their break, then handed the German naval friend the cigarette. He smiled and thanked me, then offered me a postage stamp in exchange. The face of Hitler on the stamp made me shudder. He gestured with his hands. What would I really like? I pointed to his shiny brass buttons. He took a penknife out of his pocket and cut a button from his jacket. He handed it to me, and I thought it was real gold.

On another day I wandered over to see the POWs again. They were whittling pieces of wood and out of this they made wooden acrobat figures of men somersaulting when you pressed the sticks on either side.

The men were being moved the following week, and as I was leaving my POW friend handed me his jumping man on sticks. I thought I had won a fortune. I said goodbye.

One way of finding out what people valued most was to see them attempting to retrieve their valuables from their bombed house. Fireman "Tini" Wright hurried to help a woman outside the ruin of her house in London:

SHE SAW her house had been destroyed and remarked, "Oh, well, I still have my bloody pawn ticket."

Jean Rush, who lived several miles from central London, had a bomb drop in her back garden:

WHEN THE BOMB DROPPED, the house shook, but amazingly no windows were broken, although the blackout curtains were blown down. I can remember running over the whole house turning off lights and was quite a heroine for a few days. Everyone else was too petrified to think about the blackout, but I suppose at the age of 10 I wasn't aware of what a close shave we'd had.

I remember my father and uncle (who was in the Home Guard) went out into the garden to see what had fallen. My father came back saying, "There's a hell of a hole out there!" which was a family joke for the rest of his life, as the understatement of the year. Luckily we had a long garden and my mother had made an allotment at the end of it. The ground was well dug and wet, so the bomb, a 50 pounder, had buried deep before exploding.

The main thing I remember next day, when we went out and saw the crater in the daylight, were the cabbages stuck in the row of poplar trees at the end of the garden.

Nell and Alf continued to consider themselves lucky. St George's Buildings had miraculously escaped the falling bombs, although the ever-cruising ack-ack gun along the railway tracks nearby still succeeded in breaking windows whenever it stopped to bark and throw its harmless missiles toward the enemy.

Irene Martin was 10 and had been evacuated, but she returned for a cousin's wedding and stayed:

MY FAMILY MOVED to a house which was on the border of Finsbury and the city of London.

When the blitz started we went to a local shelter, but this became too crowded and uncomfortable. Someone mentioned to my mother that there was a better shelter situated in Clerkenwell Road which was known as Foresters Hall. It was quite a deep shelter and consisted of bays, each of which had a few wooden contraptions that you could make up as beds, and also a few three-tier bunks. The shelter itself was a mass of grey concrete and always felt damp and cold.

The trek to the shelter started as soon as it got dark or when the wireless ceased broadcasting. We had bundles of bedding and odds and ends and, like refugees, would make our way. After making up our beds we would sit and talk. Lots of women took up knitting, and we would make friends with families in the other bays. There were always one or two wardens about on top to keep an eye open for any incendiary bombs and, in general, look after us.

Once the dreaded siren had sounded we tried to be normal, hoping for the best, I suppose. Eventually everyone would try to get some sleep and, being young, I suppose it was a lot easier for me. Of course we all slept in our clothes, which was horrible. And you could hear the noise going on in a muffled sort of way.

Early in the morning everyone would pack up their belongings and head for home, and the thing that stays with me is seeing miles and miles (or so it seems) of firemen's hoses lying all along the roads and the smell of burning. Once home, I used to crawl into bed for some extra sleep until it was time to get ready for school.

Whilst Mum, my two sisters and myself went to the shelter, my father insisted on staying home to look after things, although he used to check up on neighbours who refused to leave their homes.

After a while the bombing became very intense and very frightening, and in the middle of one particular night, after the all-clear had sounded, our wardens insisted we get up to look at the sight outside. We could hardly believe our eyes. The whole city seemed to be on fire and even the factory next to our shelter was burning. You can imagine how lucky we were to be so close to everything and still be safe. We really believed that the square mile of city had gone forever.

Eventually, after many weeks of the same routine, Mum had had enough, and I will never forget one Saturday night. My sisters had already gone to the shelter and Dad was creating merry hell because Mum refused to go. Well, on time as usual, the wireless went quiet, the siren sounded and over they came. The bombs started to fall and the ack-ack guns created such horrendous noise that Mum soon realized how silly she had been, so we made for the local shelter, running all the way, and we could hear the shrapnel falling about us and we were terrified. Obviously we made it all right, and the experience was never repeated.

I must tell you that apart from all the terrible things that were happening, the atmospere at Foresters Hall was fantastic. Everyone was friendly and helped others less fortunate, and there were many laughs as we listened to the elderly tell stories of their pasts. Certain things come to mind such as the night the rumour went round that a parachute had been found on top and we thought the invasion had started, and someone mentioned that a man was sitting on his own in one of the bays. Nobody had ever seen him before and we wondered if he was a spy. On tackling him, one of the wardens found out that the poor man had been caught out in the raid and had come into the shelter for safety. Incidentally, the parachute was a piece of barrage balloon that had come down.

Another incident concerned Dad, who, during a very heavy raid, tried to get an elderly spinster in our street down the shelter, whereupon she said she couldn't leave without her cat. The short answer from Dad was "Sod the cat!"

Nell continued to make her way to the Borough underground station where she could sleep away the night undisturbed by the noise above. Truth was, she and many of those who now made their nightly visit had found a new life on the station platforms. Certainly the station was far better lit than most of the homes they had left, and a party atmosphere soon began to develop with regular and new friends. It was not uncommon for a singsong to start, and since Nell was far from shy, her voice, along with the others, soon echoed through the dark empty tunnels with everything from "There's an Old Mill by the Stream, Nelly Dean" to the more modern "Bluebirds Over the White Cliffs of Dover."

Rose Headock and her husband were living in Carshalton, Surrey. They had a young daughter and son and lived in a bungalow:

THE SMALL BEDROOM was downstairs and had a triangle window. My husband sandbagged the window up and put our table-tennis table-top over the lot and fixed it to the wall. We had a mattress on the floor to sleep on. My husband's mother, who lived in Ramsgate, wrote to us and asked if she could come up and stay with us, which she did. The siren went off, my mother-in-law was sleeping on the camp bed and our son, Allan, in his cot in the lounge. We all went into the small room and stayed there until the all-clear went. Mother said she would go back to bed. I was a little uneasy walking up and down the hall with Allan in my arms.

As things seemed to have quieted down, Mother went to bed and I put Allan back in his cot. My husband, daughter and I went back to lie on the mattress. We had hardly been there a few minutes when I saw a silver light go down the boarded window. I came round later in hospital.

When my husband came to see me he told me we had lost our home. His dear mother had been killed and our son, being so small, had gone through the house and was found outside the dining-room window. He had been taken to another hospital.

I was told afterward that the plane had dropped four 500-pound bombs. The crater in our front garden and part of our home you could put two double-decker buses in. The council found us a house to live in until our first one was rebuilt in 1947.

Throughout the blitz, hospitals and emergency services were crucial. The workers and patients managed to carry on despite the odds.

Patricia Poyser had been in a London hospital for six months, suffering with typhoid:

I WAS FOUR OR FIVE at the time. My father, who was serving in the army, tells me of coming in to visit me and finding other children and myself in the hospital corridor with potties on our heads as helmets.

Pam Wood was three and suffering from hepatitis. She was unable to walk and had been transferred to the Queen Elizabeth Hospital for Sick Children in Carshalton, Surrey:

ONE NIGHT I absolutely refused to eat my bread-and-milk supper, even when they added cocoa, and as a punishment I was taken out of the main ward and put out in a side ward on my own, in complete darkness. Sometime later the air-raid warning sounded, and as usual, all the children were carried down to the air-raid shelter in the basement.

Unfortunately, as there had been a shift change of the nursing staff, I was forgotten and nobody came for me. I was unable to move as I was in a plaster cast, and by the time that I realized what was happening nobody could hear my cries.

That was the most terrifying night of my life. When I close my eyes I can still see the explosions of light and darkness, hear the whining sound as the bombs fell through the air, followed by the unmistakable thrump when they hit the ground, and then the ear-splitting sound of the explosions.

I hid under the blankets with my eyes shut tight and my hands over my ears, but could not blot out either the flames or the noise.

I felt sure that the hospital had been hit and because I had been naughty I had gone straight to hell.

Florence Heaney-Thompson had been taken to the Royal Infirmary Hospital in Liverpool for an operation on her throat:

THE NIGHT AFTER my operation a land mine dropped behind the hospital. The two very high windows, one either side of the bed, blasted inward and I was buried under iron frames, brick, woodwork and glass. The lights had failed. I was in a side ward, myself and one other patient, a much older woman, Miss Dees, whom they managed to get out. Sisters and nurses in tin helmets, carrying storm lamps, were unable to cross the floor to help me, as it was too dangerous. They sent for St. John's Ambulance men.

Window frames, bricks and rubble were moved off my bed (those men were wonderful — cheery and talking to me all the time); however, they were not able to lift me out with bedclothes. To their astonishment I was pinned to the bed with long slivers of glass. Eventually I was lifted above the glass and placed on a stretcher. Would you believe I didn't have a scratch or a cut on me?!

Florence Cunnington was a probationary nurse in an emergency hospital in Hendon that was bombed three times:

THE FIRST ONE hit the dispensary and destroyed most things there. The second fell on one of the wards, killing five children, two of whom belonged to one couple. The third hit the lodge building and destroyed it.

I remember well the nights when the sirens went. We slept in the long air-raid shelter built for us, sisters in the first part, staff nurses farther down, and then came us probationers.

When I went on duty one morning, one poor old gent said, "You are a fine lot of nurses." I said, "Why?" He said that when he was calling for the bedpan, a nurse crept out from under his bed.

Joan Gates (now Stone) had been transferred to the air-raid casualty department in the Southern Hospital in Dartford, Kent:

A STRETCHER CASE arrived with his head bandaged. I asked the ambulance man if it was a "head case." The casualty promptly sat up and said, "Far from it, Nurse." He thought I had said "dead"!

One night, I recall, when the raids were heavy I was on the men's ward. I was as frightened as anybody, but of course could never show fear. I used to sit by the side of little boys who were in bed and hold their hands. To help both of us!

Joyce Smith was 10 years old and in a hospital in Bath having her tonsils removed:

THE SIRENS SOUNDED and at first none of the staff or children in the ward seemed very frightened. The aircraft noises and bombing came much closer, and suddenly there was a mighty explosion in the grounds of the hospital. The glass walls of the ward shattered and we were left in the open air. The nurses very quickly put several of us into one big iron hospital cot and wheeled us to a lift where we were taken to a new and very crowded ward. Two or three other other cots followed us into the ward. All night long while the bombing continued and the overworked nurses attended to the patients, I amazed the twin toddlers who were in the cot with me. I sang to them, played "walkie round the garden" and "this little piggy," and told them stories until morning. My father drove a furniture van that could be used as an ARP ambulance, so when he heard about the hospital bombing, he put up his ambulance sign and drove the 13 miles to Bath, being allowed through restricted areas because of his "ambulance." He collected me from the hospital, and although I was not due for discharge I was allowed to go home. The nurses were full of praise for his "courageous little girl," but my nervous system paid a high price for this during the following months.

Two things I shall never forget about that journey home were the shattered homes and weary dirty people scratching for belongings or relatives. Also the fact that my father had managed to get some chocolate for me and I was unable to eat it because of my swollen sore throat.

Most first-aid workers had dozens of grim encounters. Mrs. Bard was with a first-aid unit working in London during the heaviest of the raids:

AN OIL BOMB sheared the foot off a man except for a small piece of skin on the heel. Blood was spurting freely when the first-aid party arrived and the leader immediately applied a tourniquet. He was then debating how to bandage the wound effectively because of the detached skin, when an onlooker said that it should be cut off.

The first-aid man hesitated and the onlooker then produced a card which said he was a doctor and offered to do the job. This was accepted and done and the stump then bandaged by the leader and the victim laid on a stretcher under a blanket to wait the arrival of the ambulance.

On clearing up, the first-aid leader realized that he had a boot with a foot in it to be disposed of. This was settled by putting it under the blanket and sending it to the hospital with the owner.

In a square near Bayswater a bomb dropped on a block of flats, slicing through the middle and leaving four floors visible from the street. The first-aid party waiting for Heavy Rescue to do their bit were suddenly surprised to see a woman on the top floor sit up in a bed. Despite the danger, one of the first-aid workers dashed into the building to bring her down. If she had got out of the bed on her left side she would have trod on nothing and landed four floors below. Instead she chose the right side, put on a pair of glasses and dressing gown and walked through a door. The first-aid worker met her and helped her down.

She'd certainly got out the right side of the bed on this occasion.

A bomb dropped on Paddington station and trapped a man behind a huge pile of debris. A small opening was made — it couldn't be too large because of the danger of collapse — and the man was told to lie down, and put his arms through the opening so he could be dragged through.

He was told to be perfectly still while this was being done, but he ignored the warning and twisted from side to side. Just as he came through the opening he twisted and drove a nail through the side of his head. He died on the way to hospital.

We must have got rather callous after a time. Clearing up after an incident to make sure we had cleared the site of dead and wounded, one of our party called out, "Here's a pair of legs!" The rest dashed over. The finder held up a pair of doll's legs and said, "I can't find the rest of the body."

Hundreds, often those on their way home from work, continued to watch the night-time spectacle overhead as searchlights lit the sky. Despite the danger, many cabs continued to operate; so did the tea wagons that stood at major intersections and served their customers regardless of what was happening above. Even the buses carried on and stopped only to allow passengers to take cover if the bombing appeared to be getting particularly heavy.

It was 7 A.M. as Nell left the bank and made her way across London Bridge toward home. Most of the city had begun crawling from their shelters to start a new day. Hitler's bombers, knowing that their cover of darkness was fast disappearing, had usually gone and were by then on their way back to their bases. The Borough market was alive with venders tossing the fruit and vegtables onto carts and comparing the ferocity of the previous night's raid. The coffee stall that stood at the foot of the bridge was a perfect meeting place. Most of the regulars nodded and gave Nell a "Wot cher, Nell" as she hurried by.

Henry Jackson was with Associated Press and was on his way by bus to his office in London when an air-raid warning sounded.

THE CONDUCTOR took a mouth organ from his pocket and marched the passengers off the bus to a nearby shelter, leading the way with renditions of "Tipperary" and "Pack Up Your Troubles in Your Old Kit Bag and Smile."

Nevertheless, transportation to and from work remained a problem, perhaps one of the biggest, to many. Jay Hacking was 18, and getting to work was certainly his major problem:

AS THE BOMBING intensified it became harder and harder to reach the office each day. We did our best, sometimes taking longer to do the journeys than we spent at the office and travelling on all kinds of unlikely vehicles, including flat-top lorries.

The Germans had the habit of dropping high-explosive bombs on the railway lines, which meant that the trains drove as far as the crater, all the passengers got out and either walked or were ferried by bus to the other side of it and completed the journey in another train. Much the same thing used to happen with the trams, and only the buses were able to find ways round the gaps. Parachuted land mines were another hazard; the areas around New Cross seemed to be a favourite target and a great deal of devastation was caused there by them.

On at least one occasion an exploded mine got caught in the telegraph wires near New Cross station, which caused even more chaos for the commuters. It was safely dealt with by the bomb-disposal unit.

For those fighting the war at sea there was no guarantee that their port of arrival would be a safe haven. Signalman Eric Willie was on a destroyer that put into Portsmouth on the day following an air raid:

THE OFF-DUTY members of the crew were split into pairs. Each pair was provided with a stirrup pump, a bucket and small axe and sent ashore as firefighting parties to deal with the second night of air-raid fires.

I was paired with wireless telegraphist Peter Webster; we were sent to Kings Road, Southsea. When we arrived, Kings Road seemed to be ablaze from end to end. As we walked along the road, a policeman dismounted from his bicycle and said, "Are you a fire-fighting party?" "Yes!" we said. "Then get on with it!" he said.

I explained that with our modest equipment we needed to find a small fire. He rode off in disgust. The only noise was of fire and partial collapse of houses. The people were in shelters and there were no exploding bombs. All the damage that night was caused by incendiary bombs, as far as we could see.

We spotted a house with smoke coming from the eaves. After a lot of banging on the door, a very pale lady answered and said that her husband was out seeing a patient and that we must find another doctor. We persuaded her to come to the pavement to see the smoke coming from her house. She reluctantly allowed us into the house (young sailors were not highly regarded).

Peter filled the bath with cold water and I climbed into the roof space. It was filthy and full of smoke, a faint glow was visible at a point where the roof met the wall and there was a clean hole in the roof just over my head. The doctor's wife passed the nozzle of the pump to me, Peter started pumping and I was able to direct a small stream of water at the bomb.

In a short while the glow disappeared, steam mingled with the smoke and I called to Peter to stop pumping and started to lower myself through the hatch. After I'd gone about three rungs down the ladder both my legs were firmly grasped. Our policeman friend had decided to take charge. "Get back up there and finish the job," he said. "It is finished and I'm coming down," I said. The doctor's wife was repeatedly asking, "What's going on?" and Peter was telling the policeman to let me go.

As soon as I reached the floor the policeman grabbed the hose end and ascended the ladder to finish the job. He was a big man and quite unable to get through the hatch. He ordered me to get into the roof and follow his instructions. I refused to do so. Peter was equally uncooperative, so the policeman placed us under arrest.

We were taken to Portsmouth Police Station and questioned and put in a cell. Peter was telling me his opinion (worth listening to since he was a solicitor in civilian life) about whether we would be safer in prison than on the high seas when we heard the familiar voice of our captain demanding our immediate release and making the sort of remarks we would've liked to have made to our custodians.

Lilian Nesta Kerslake (now Smith) was nine when the war started and was living with her parents on the outskirts of Plymouth. The city was bombed on March 21 and 22, 1941. Her mother had taken her to the city for a church service that was over at 8 P.M.:

WE COULD NOT LEAVE the building as there was a lot of bombing and the streets were ablaze with fires. After a while a bomb was dropped near to where we were, and the building fell in on us. My mother took me by the hand and pulled me out of the rubble, and we ran down the road looking for an air-raid shelter. Eventually an air-raid warden told us to go into the Charles Street Church shelter, which I can remember was very crowded and dark.

In that shelter I heard people saying that a bomb had been dropped very near to us. We'd felt the blast round our legs, but had this blast passed higher we would have died because our lungs would have collapsed.

Dorothy Marshall was in the middle of Plymouth when the bombs began to fall:

THERE WAS a lovely smell of roast pork coming from the shop on whose window-sill I was sitting. It was minutes before I realized that the shop was a delicatessen and it was blazing behind me.

Ten-year-old Billy Clark was with his family during the bombing of Plymouth:

THE TIME WAS 7:35 P.M. Mother told me to turn on the radio as there was a program she wanted to listen to that started at 8 P.M. From the radio came the terrible noise of static, and nothing of the program could be heard. "Turn it off," said Mum. "We'll try again later."

At 8 o'clock she turned it on again. This time a man's voice was screaming, "Take cover, take cover! There are hundreds of them." A few seconds later the sirens started wailing. Mother said to Aunt Jessie, "Take Billy and Cynthia to the shelter. I'll get Jean and follow on." Jean was in bed asleep.

We put on our overcoats (we always put on overcoats when going to the shelter, whatever the weather) and Cynthia was first out of the door followed by me and Aunt Jessie carrying the bags of extra bits and pieces to take to the shelter — cushions, blankets and a hot drink if there was time to make one.

We ran to the shelter, which was about 200 yards away in another street. We had been trained to keep close to the walls of the buildings in the street and to pause in doorways every 20 yards or so to let the grown-ups catch up.

We reached the shelter — at least they called it a shelter. It was actually the basement of a three- or four-storey warehouse which had been reinforced with brick internal walls. The air-raid warden recognized us as regulars and said, "Come on in, son. You know the way." Eventually I went to sleep.

I awoke suddenly to noise and confusion. I felt heavy pressure all over me. We had been bombed and were now buried. I tried to force myself through the rubble but I didn't have the strength.

The only thing I could do was move my right forefinger. I don't know how long we were buried because I drifted in and out of consciousness. Eventually I awoke to find that my legs were cold. I had been partially uncovered by the rescue workers. I had the sense to move my legs from side to side to attract attention to myself. I felt a hand on my knee and heard a man's comforting voice saying, "All right, son. We know you're there." A few minutes later the rescuers finished digging me out and carried me to an ambulance. I remember being surprised at finding that the ambulance driver was a young woman. I thought only men could drive.

There were no doors on the back of the ambulance. I was on one of four stretchers strapped in for safety. As we drove through the streets of Plymouth I could see that the whole sky was lit up by the fires on the ground. We were driven through burning streets and frequently bumped over bits of rubble. Our young driver found her way through all the damage and confusion to the hospital. The last thing I remembered was a man with a bald head bending over me saying, "Hello, son. What's wrong with you?"

While my rescue was taking place, Mum and Cynthia had been taken to another shelter a few yards from the one we were in.

Sometime later there was a lull in the bombing. Mum and Cynthia made their way out of the shelter to go home for a cup of tea. As they got to the door, an officious air-raid warden said, "You can't go back in there yet. The all-clear hasn't gone."

Mum, who was only about five foot three, grabbed hold of the front of the man's uniform and said, "Listen, you! I have just had my sister killed in that shelter over the road, my five-year-old daughter went as well, and I don't even know where my son is." Still shaking the man by his coat, she continued, "I am going into my home for a cup of tea, and you and nobody else is going to stop me."

(I was told later that Aunt Jessie had been killed outright by the bomb, and my sister had been alive for a while but the dust of the rubble covered her head and she suffocated.)

Of the 22 persons in the shelter, 11 died, three of them babies in prams.

Nine members of the family of Ursula Paula Beaven (now Bullen) were killed in the Plymouth blitz in March 1941:

THE BOMBING had gone on for five nights with the warning siren sounding at 7:25 to the minute every night. That in itself was infuriating.

After school on the fateful day — I was then 15 — I accompanied my great-aunt to take tea at the home of my mother's oldest brother, William, as her younger brother, Francis, had sustained a broken leg in a public house which had been bombed the previous evening. I promised to join my uncle Frank and travel to the hospital in a taxi the following morning. We left the house about 6:45 P.M. in order to reach home by the prescribed time for the air raids.

The next day I set out to keep my morning appointment and on the way met another of my mother's brothers, Uncle Bart, his wife, 18-month-old twin sons and five-year-old daughter at an in-law's house. Everyone threw their arms around me and cried. After a period of time I realized they were telling me their house had been burned down by incendiary bombs and they had escaped. At the tail end of the raid they had walked through the devastation to William's house, only to find it in ruins after a direct hit.

At the behest of Uncle Bart I went down to William's house to tell the men who were digging exactly who was in the house at tea-time the previous day.

When I reached my destination I saw my cousin Sheila's fur coat hanging over the telegraph wires across the street. This coat was later returned to the family. Winding my way through a small group of people, I was recognized by one of the men digging in the ruins. He knew my mother and her brothers. I noted only one part of a wall was standing, on which was a shelf holding a glass bowl which contained eggs, some unbroken.

I gave the men the required information and left. On looking over my shoulder some moments later, I saw the rescue man still standing on the same spot as if rooted. The tears were pouring down his begrimed face.

Marjorie Ulph (now Davidson) was sitting in a concrete shelter in the back garden of her Hull home when the bombs started to drop:

WE HEARD THEM whistling down and we used to say, "This one isn't for us as we can hear it whistling." When it did hit the ground the earth would rock.

When we came out of the shelter and saw all the damage, there was a big gap at the corner of the street where seven people lost their lives.

My aunt, who lived at Dennington, near Sheffield, saw a huge red glow in the sky and was told that it was Hull on fire. My aunt took a train to Hull and walked through the wreckage to our house (no buses). When she took one look at my mother, she burst into tears, saying, "I never thought I'd see you alive again."

Murial Winnie Keymer, of Rugby, was asleep with her husband by her side when she awoke with a start. She asked her husband if they could go home to see if anything had happened to her parents. He assured her they would and both went back to sleep:

IN THE MORNING I heard that a town in East Anglia had been bombed. I knew. It was not until the Wednesday that the telegram arrived: "48 demolished. No Trace."

It seemed incredible that this could happen to me. We went immediately and found the train full with forces going home on compassionate leave. The naval people found me a seat and a cup of tea. A petty officer asked me where I was bound for and I showed him the telegram.

Arriving at Norwich, we met my brother. He was in the army, and together we walked to my sister's home — quite a distance. The searchlights were up and we knew another raid was imminent. It came as we got to my sister's house, and the six of us crouched under a Morrison shelter. The bombing started, the ground shook and I prayed to die. The raid seemed to last for hours and we eventually, with the help of an air-raid warden, dragged ourselves out.

Outside were men from all over the country, their fire hoses trailing in the streets. All my sister's windows were blown out and filled with brown material, and tanks called round with fresh water, which had to be boiled.

As soon as possible we went to see if our parents, sister and niece had been found, and when I saw my old home flattened and rescue workers digging the rubble I was too tired to cry.

Finally I went to the city hall to see the town clerk to ascertain what teams had been at work there. Despite much opposition I succeeded in finding the assistant town clerk, who knew me, and eventually I found the bodies of my parents — or rather, my mother had been found. Alfred eventually found my baby niece — her neck had been broken. My sister he identified by her hands. My mother was in a bag labelled "Elderly lady with hair going grey." My father they never found. Although the roofs were searched for weeks after, they eventually buried only an arm.

A letter from Nell's son mentioned that he would soon be home. At 14 he was old enough to go to work. Would he stay in the buildings with Alf or join her on the Borough station platform? Certainly the extra pair of hands would prove useful in carrying the bedclothes to

the shelter. Or better yet, the raids might be over by then. Whatever
happened, it would be lovely to have him home again.

The bombing of London was far from over. On March 19 the
Luftwaffe was back again in even bigger numbers. They left
behind 750 dead.

Elsie Noades lived over a shop in Hampstead:

THE PREMISES RECEIVED a direct hit. My son and I were
buried for 21 hours — from 1 A.M. Friday to 9 A.M. Saturday.
He was three and half years old at the time. I remember coming
to and feeling him by my side, impressing on him to keep his
eyes shut. He didn't though, and consequently was blind for
four days — the debris had got into his eyes. My legs were
trapped and I had a nail in my forehead which I managed to
wriggle out. Anyway, if it had not been for my mum and dad I'd
have been there now. Fire broke out and there was a gas explosion. The warden said no one could survive under these conditions. My parents insisted that I must be there because normally
I would light a fire for them and do a little shopping and had I
gone anywhere I would have left a note. The next morning a
hundred men were put on the site and began digging. I was
found at 9 A.M. My first words were, "What time is it?"
Everybody cheered as my son and I were brought out.

In spite of the air raids life went along much as it always had.
Mrs. Lynton was six and her sister nine when they found, much to
their sorrow, that school changed very little:

ONE DAY we were sent home from school because a land mine
had fallen in the grounds but had not exploded. We were disappointed when it was disarmed safely. We'd thought we had the
chance of a holiday if the school blew up.

If the siren went during school hours we would go to the shelters and continue our lessons there, though they were usually in

the form of spelling bees, mental arithmetic, quizzes and singsongs. If the all-clear had not gone by the end of the morning or afternoon classes, we were not allowed to go home unless an adult had come to collect us.

My mother would collect us, putting up her umbrella to keep off any falling shrapnel, and we would all march home quite confident of its ability to protect us.

The children would go shrapnel gathering in the morning. Bits of shrapnel were popular collector's pieces and were swopped for comics, small toys and things. Everybody hoped to find the tail fins of incendiary bombs, which were reputed to be of fabulous value. I never saw any tail fins, and to be honest am not sure that they existed, or alternatively that they survived the fire that the bomb caused.

The teenage daughter of a neighbour was in the garden when an incendiary bomb landed near her but did not ignite on landing. She tried to disable it by putting a dustbin lid on top, but this made it explode, causing a lot of damage. She was reported in *The Daily Mirror* because of this. We all thought she was stupid — we knew that you were supposed to put earth or sand on an incendiary bomb, and all I could think of was that it was a waste of a good tail fin.

Jean Hewitt (now Emmins) was 13 and had returned to London after being evacuated:

FATHER WAS in a reserve occupation at Tooting, and Mum was called to a munitions factory at Earlsfield. Even though we never knew if we'd be together again, in the evening we all went about our affairs in a relatively light-hearted manner, never hugging or kissing each other goodbye. It was surprising how life went on in spite of the war. I went to the cinema regularly and most Saturday nights I went dancing at the Streatham Locarno.

June Smith (now Harmer) was seven during the blitz, and living with her sister and parents in Hackney, east London:

EACH NIGHT we went to the public shelter where we slept in three-tier bunk beds. There was row upon row of them in the basement of this furniture shop. Dad slept in the top bunk, my sister in the bottom one and Mum and I in the middle. We would go to the shelter as soon as we had eaten our tea, and Dad would join us when he got home. Some nights he didn't come home as he was in his company's fire brigade and was often on night duty.

During breaks in the raids we would go across the road to a café by the Hackney Empire to get a jug of tea. If the siren went while you were queuing up you had to decide whether to give up your place in the queue and take shelter, or take a chance and get your tea.

During the blitz, the King and Queen juggled their time between London and the relative safety of Windsor. They frequently made trips to areas to give the residents encouragement. Sarah Cartwright had gone to a theatre in the West End to celebrate her mother's seventy-fifth birthday:

NEAR THE END of the performance the siren went and they announced that the show would go on, but advised people in the balcony to come downstairs and they would entertain us all until the all-clear sounded.

We decided to stay and enjoy the singsong that followed, but when things seemed to quiet down outside we thought we would make for the underground and wend our way home to Kennington. We had just started our trek to the tube when the barrage started up again, so we hurried down the air-raid shelter in Piccadilly.

We hadn't been there very long before three men in tin hats and uniforms came running down the steps. One of them was the King. He came round and spoke to us all and complimented my mother on her courage at venturing out, and when she told him it was her birthday he wished her many happy returns.

After a while the bombs were still raining down and the air-raid warden who accompanied the King said he had to leave as he would be needed. The King said, "Just a minute and I'll be with you," and the warden said, "But sir, it's too dangerous for you. I'm going because it's my job." The King replied, "It is my job too!"

Different people had different fears. Pam Gibbons (now Buckland) lived in southwest London:

MUM'S PERSONAL FEAR was that the house would fall about her ears as she sat on the "lav" or took a bath, and these essential operations were carried out at high speed. I was more afraid that I might see a dead person, or worse, half a dead person, after a neighbour related the grisly story of seeing the lower part of a man standing at his garden gate — no one asked where the rest of him was.

John Barber was 11 and living in the Hackney Marshes. The marsh was used as a dumping ground for much of the debris resulting from the bombing and was a perfect place to explore for discarded "treasures":

WHEN REEVES AND SONS, the famous artists' materials suppliers, was bombed we found a wonderful selection of paint, watercolours and inks all in very good condition. We had to move very carefully just to salvage it as the lorries continued tipping and at times it could be dangerous. These materials were a prize for me and my pal, Wally.

Hester Stephens (now Wood) was a schoolgirl living in Sunbury-on-Thames. She had arrived at the railway station to catch the train to school only to find that it had received a direct hit in the night:

THE IMMEDIATE REACTION of my fellow passengers and myself was that of rejoicing — we wouldn't be able to get to school. Then we found that the Southern Railway had set up a bus shuttle to the next station, Hampton, where we could easily walk to school.

The city gents with their bowler hats, pin-striped trousers and inevitable rolled-up umbrellas claimed all the seats, and we girls, clad in our nunlike grey wool, clutching lunches and grey gym knickers, swayed in the aisle.

At Hampton everyone filed off the bus. We girls gathered in a little group, deciding what was to be done to delay facing incarceration as long as possible, when a gentleman, impeccably dressed for town, caught our attention. He suddenly started searching his pockets, at first calmly, then in desperation, looking for his handkerchief, which he failed to find. Then he let out an ear-splitting, uncontrolled sneeze. But, oh, horror! With the sneeze a complete set of dentures flew through the air as if jet-propelled and landed in the gutter.

The bus driver decided to back his bus out of the station yard and the poor city gent stood paralyzed with horror as the bus ran over his dentures and then forward again to adjust for a better turn. He gave a little cry of despair and did a feeble little leap in the air, then disappeared into the gents' cloakroon.

Many people were bombed out more than once. Marion Eason's mother lost three homes, and each time she walked about the streets with an old wheelbarrow or pram, salvaging what she could.

I WAS BORN in February 1941. In the same year we lost our first home in an air raid, and I caught diptheria at 10 months of age.

Dad was serving in the Royal Navy, fighting abroad most of the time. Mum, being a true Cockney, was one of 14 children. Poverty was a natural part of life for her and her family. But their poverty-stricken lives helped them survive.

Mum said she used to get a really bad feeling just before she was bombed out — like a premonition, I suppose. The first time I was only a baby, and Mum says she had this awful feeling that something was going to happen. She got me all ready, sat me in the pram while she got her bits and pieces together. She left the pram at the house and carried me across London to visit her brother.

There was no transport running, and as she walked there was an air raid. She must have found shelter somewhere.

The next day my dad came home on leave. He went to the house and found it as flat as a pancake.

Edith Dowse was born in Holborn. A true Londoner, she was bombed out four times. The first time was at Queens Road, Wimbledon:

WE BACKED onto the railway line, which was used for pompom guns going up and down the line during the raids. The town hall at the bottom of the road was used as an air-raid shelter. During the many daytime raids and alerts, this was quite a meeting place for local mums with children to congregate. We grabbed our babies and our knitting and dashed for the shelter.

I was rushing past the town hall with my son in his pram one day when the warden shouted to me to take cover. I had only a hundred yards to go and wanted to get home. He dragged me and the pram under cover just in time, because when I got home the babies' nappies looked like colanders.

Our next move took us to West Hill, Wandsworth. Our flat was in a large house next to the art college. Soldiers had been billeted but had now vacated the premises — but they forgot to tell Hitler. Dozens of bombs rained down one night and more were dropped at the top of the hill where a building housed a great number of Americans.

We were got out, given a cup of tea and sat on the pavement. A pitch-dark night lit up like day with fires and buildings in flames. Once again we were re-housed but left some of our good furniture in storage. A rosewood piano was left for three years, and when we retrieved it and unlocked it we found that the inside was missing, presumably blown out.

Times were difficult enough for those who were healthy. Anyone like Margaret Townsend's grandmother, though, had the additional problem of being in a wheelchair:

BECAUSE OF THIS she always insisted that when there was an air raid she would stay under the stairs of the house, as it was too much for my mother to lift both her and the chair down to the shelter. Mum, having settled my grandmother, took me with her down to the shelter in the garden.

Sometime later a bomb exploded at the side of the house. As Mum and I came out of the shelter it was like being in a thick fog. I can remember hearing my mother scream, "Are you safe, Mum?" When the dust started to clear my grandmother was in her chair calling back that she was all right. A small part of the wall beside her was intact and hanging from it was a glass-framed picture of myself which had not been damaged at all.

My mother, who was completely shocked by this experience, said to me, "I'll find somewhere for the two of us to have a drink." She had never been to a public house before on her own, but we found a pub and in the two of us went. We sat with our drinks in our hands, our faces as black as coal. We must have looked a strange sight.

Paul Wilks attended the local "infants" school in Swindon. The school was well prepared for air raids, and staff and students were constantly practising:

MRS. WILLIAMS, the headmistress, would tell us that she was going to ring the bell, and when we heard it we were to make our way to the shelter. The real thing occurred one afternoon during classes. Our teacher, Miss Hitchin, told us to follow her to the shelter. I remember thinking at the time, Why didn't silly old Miss Williams tell us she was going to ring the bell, the way she had done in the past?

With her younger sister, Patricia, who was two and a half, eight-year-old Maureen Jones (now Renshaw) lived close to an aircraft factory. When the bombing began they were forced to go to a public shelter close by:

AS THE SIRENS SOUNDED my aunt and mum used to put the youngest children in their prams — one at each end — place the old tin baths over the tops and run like hell across to the shelter.

Doris Monk's married sister and her husband owned a butcher shop in north London:

THE BOMBING had been very bad there for several weeks. My sister kept saying, "Oh, for a good night's sleep, properly in your pyjamas." They she and her husband had an opportunity to spend the weekend in the country away from it all, in a caravan at Waltham Cross.

They duly went. The first night a bomb fell in the same field as the caravan, blew them completely out of bed, out of the caravan and into the field, complete in their pyjamas. My sister was more scared of the cows than the bombs!

John Norris's father, Charles (Charlie) Norris, was the local ARP watchkeeper/ambulance driver. Although they were living in the countryside they had experienced bombing from attacks on nearby Swansea:

AN ALERT WAS CALLED, there was an air raid imminent, so Dad sounded the siren. He became concerned as to how my mother would cope with me and my grandmother who lived with us. In a state of rising anxiety, he ran through the darkened streets to our house. As he had feared, my mother was quite agitated, trying to dress a squalling child and trying to persuade Gran to come to the shelter, while at the same time getting together blankets and a little food to take with us in case the alert was long and drawn out, as they often were.

Gran settled her side of the argument by locking herself in the stair cupboard with her savings and pension books, a few precious possessions and Dad's shop takings for the week stowed inside a large copper kettle.

Hurriedly my mother and father gathered what was needed into a bundle, and my mother set off down the street, leaving this, while my father, having strapped me into my folding push chair, set off, pushing me in this after her.

It was dark. So dark that Dad ran me at full tilt into a lamppost. He went sprawling and my carriage and I spun off into the pitch-black night. Desperation. Time was running out and he could hear the drone of approaching aircraft. How did he find me? "Bawl!" my father used to say. "I'd have heard him above the sound of the siren." There I was. Upside down in the middle of the street strapped in the push chair and bawling like a bull. Dad gathered me up and ran with me still upside down in the push chair to the town hall and practically hurled me down the steps into the dimly lit basement among the folk who had already settled there.

My parents were resigned to the possibility that Gran had "copped it." Why, oh, why didn't the stubborn old thing come to the refuge with us? At first light came the all-clear. Father had to go off to sound it while Mum and I set out to see what was left of our home. It was still there, minus its windows and sundry slates and fittings, but substantially intact.

Gran? Gran was curled up on a rug in the stair cupboard, sound asleep. She woke up with the steely dignity she always possessed and made us a cup of tea, but only after restoring the valuable items she had clutched through the night to their rightful places.

In April, Coventry was once again chosen as the target. Doreen Robbins, who was 10, had taken cover under the stairs with her two older brothers:

MY MOTHER was puttering about in the kitchen as she always was. My father had built a little bed underneath the stairs. We went under there when the bombing was on, though we had an Anderson shelter in the garden and a Morrison shelter we didn't use, either. The dog used the Morrison as a kennel and we never went out into the Anderson because it was always full of water. Then we heard this big one coming and my mother dived under the stairs with us. The house was demolished. It took the wardens and firemen about half an hour to get us out, including the dog. A fireman carried me out over his shoulder through the bombing and the dog followed. He ran through the streets and left me in another shelter all by myself. My uncle, who was also a fireman, found me and took me back to my parents. My father, who was working for the railroad at the time, had come back and found the house demolished and of course thought we were all gone. So he just sat outside on the pavement crying.

Most people are under the impression that as their country was neutral territory, the Irish did not suffer the hardships experienced by the rest of Britain. Nothing could be further from the truth. Unlike Eire, Northern Ireland was in the war and making just as many sacrifices as anyone else.

In April 1940, Belfast received a terrible pounding. During the raid fire engines from their southern neighbour raced across the boundary between the two countries to help.

Nell sat and watched as her young son ate the rice pudding she had specially prepared for his homecoming. The family was together once more. Alf reminded them that they would miss their space in the underground station if they didn't hurry. And now they needed an extra space, but not for long.... Within hours of being part of the mass of humanity sheltering along the platform, Nell's son was throwing up. As soon as the last train had gone through, pushing fresh air into the tunnel, the stench from the open latrine buckets took over and proved too much for the young lad just back from breathing in the fresh air of the countryside.

It was the one and only time the boy accompanied his mother and sisters to the shelter. From that day on Alf had the company of his son as they lay in their beds listening to the thud of the falling bombs. For Alf, who had experienced life in the trenches of France, the sound did little to disturb his sleep. But each blast and shake of the buildings sent the terrified boy scurrying to his father's bed, only to be greeted by loud snores — not exactly the kind of reassuring sounds needed by a youngster searching for comfort during an air raid.

The night raids in Britain continued through the spring and climaxed in a shocking raid on London on May 10. With the raid expanded to cover a much larger area, the casualty figures reached a record high. Some of Britain's most majestic buildings — the House of Commons, Westminster Abbey, the Tower of London, the Law Courts and the Royal Mint — were hit and badly damaged.

Pearl Sunshine lived with her husband and parents in a large Edwardian house in London. She was in her twenties and had been married a year. Her husband was in uniform but stationed in London. She remembers the last big raid on the capital:

I HAD GREAT FAITH in our solid old house and was determined to stay in it at night whenever the sirens sounded. So my husband had brought our bed down to the basement and there we slept. On the night of the big May raid my husband, with some sixth sense, advised me to sleep in my clothes, as he thought it was going to be a bad night. I took his advice and still remember the clothes I wore to bed that night — a yellow roll-neck sweater and beige corduroy trousers. My parents had departed for Liberty's shelter, and my husband and I went to bed as usual.

I don't know exactly what time it was, but I think it was late, perhaps 11 or 12 o'clock, when we heard this enormous explosion and the windows were blown into the room and the blackout curtains hurled across to the other side. I thought the shock had made me cry and that there were tears rolling down my cheeks, but actually scores of tiny fragments of glass had embedded themselves into my face, eyelids, ears and hair, and it was blood that was trickling down my face.

At the same time we heard horrendous bangs taking place within the house. Everything from the top of the house had fallen to the bottom and we were literally entombed in our basement room.

Even fully dressed I was shivering, but my husband was absolutely wonderful. He found my shoes and coat and his own shoes and, taking me by the hand, hauled me up the pile of furniture, bricks and rubble to a little space that he could see had not been filled. We made it to the ground floor and what was left of the front of the house.

Although the middle of the night, it was as light as day from the fires raging in the vicinity of Tottenham Court Road and even nearer.

A passing taxi stopped and the driver called out, "You look in a bad way, miss. Get in the taxi — I'm taking this young lady and baby to the hospital." My husband and I got into the taxi. The young woman was in her nightdress and the driver took us to the Temperance Hospital in Hampstead Road. I was placed on a stretcher and the pieces of glass were extracted from my face with tweezers. I remember distinctly lots of pieces of glass falling out of my long hair, which dangled over the edge of the stretcher as I was being carried into the hospital. My husband had disappeared and I found out later that he had gone up to the roof of the hospital and was helping to put out fire bombs.

The final tally that night was almost 1500 killed, the largest number in one night of any raid. Thousands were without gas or water.

When the gas was cut to St. George's Buildings, Nell found herself racing around looking for candles. Her success almost resulted in the place being burned down when Alf leaned a bit too close to get a better light for reading his evening newspaper. The report that 100,000 pounds worth of gin had been destroyed was grim. Both agreed that whatever happened, Grannie Wicks should be kept from news like this since it would surely give her a heart attack.

May 10, 1941, the date of the last major air raid on London, signalled the end of the blitz. Throughout it all, the Nells and Alfs had pulled together. Some spoke of them as heroes because they "stuck it out." The reality was that most stayed to suffer the bombings because they had no choice. Where would they go? To friends in the country? To relatives overseas?

Those in the danger areas had lived in a decades-old network of relatives and friends who were impossible to replace. They were anxious to get to their places of employment, but it was not "to do their bit." For years they had been conditioned to always get to work on time because just minutes could result in unemployment or a cut in the size of the wage packet. The workplace was also, for many, a second home, and a comforting place to discuss the narrow escapes of the night before.

The people who have stuck it out have not been confined only to Britain. Ordinary people have had no choice but to make the best of it, whether living in France, Germany, Russia or Poland. They live on today in Beirut, South Africa, Belfast — everywhere that governments allow front lines to be drawn through their homes.

EPILOGUE

"**I**N 1940 AND 1941, approximately 43,000 civilians in Britain were killed by bombs. About half of all deaths (nearly 30,000) were in London. The total number of people injured more or less seriously is impossible to state exactly. If it is said that about 86,000 were seriously injured and went to hospital, and about 151,000 people were slightly injured, this is probably an underestimate." — Angus Calder, *The People's War*

Nell Wicks, my mother, died at Carpenters Park, in a senior citizens' home just outside Watford, England, in 1984. She was 93.

Alf Wicks, my father, died quietly in his sleep in 1978, at the age of 86.

Grannie Wicks died in 1940, just four months short of her one-hundredth birthday.

Doll and Howard Talbot, my sister and brother-in-law, are retired and living in the Midlands of England. They have three sons, all married, one living in Germany, one in Australia and one in Hertfordshire. They have several grandchildren.

Nan and John Hill, my other sister and brother-in-law, are retired and living in Blackheath, London. They have two married children and one grandchild.

BIBLIOGRAPHY

Bullock, Alan. *Hitler. A Study in Tyranny*. London: Penquin Books, 1952.

Calder, Angus. *The People's War*. London: Jonathan Cape Ltd., 1969.

Croall, Jonathan. *Don't You Know There's a War On?* London: Hutchinson Radius, 1989.

Harrisson, Tom. *Living through the Blitz*. London: Collins, 1976.

Irving, David. *Churchill's War*. Bullsbrook, Australia: Veritas Pub. Co., 1987.

Johnson, David. *The London Blitz*. New York: Stein and Day, 1981.

Mack, Joanna, and Steve Humphries. *London at War*. London: Sidgwick and Jackson, 1985.

Marwick, Arrhur. *The Home Front*. London: Thames and Hudson, 1976.

Middleton, Drew. *The Sky Suspended*. London: Longmans Green and Co., 1960.

Nicolson, Nigel, ed. *Diaries and Letters of Harold Nicholson*, Vol. 2. New York: Atheneum, 1967.

Perry, Colin. *Boy in the Blitz*. London: Leo Cooper, 1972.

ACKNOWLEDGEMENTS

WHEN IT WAS suggested that I write this book, my first reaction was surprise. To collect the stories needed from those who lived through the blitz on Britain in 1940-1941 I felt would be an impossible task.

I was wrong. With the help of many newspaper editors, my appeal to readers with stories to tell resulted in more than a thousand letters. Without them, *Nell's War* would have remained just another book idea.

My sisters, Doll and Nan, filled in the blanks of my childhood spent in Southwark, and the many new friends I found during my trips into the East End of London told me their stories.

The former Allied and German pilots who so readily gave of their time, and my editors, Charis Wahl and Maryan Gibson in Canada and Penny Phillips in England, who shuffled the words and pages, must also be thanked, along with Robin Fawcett, my remarkable researcher.

Once again my wife, Doreen, showed endless patience, and last but far from least, a loving and kind mother and father made *Nell's War* possible.

Do you remember V–E Day 1945?

Almost 50 years ago the Second World War ended in Europe. As the last sounds of the victory parades faded, men and women by the thousands faced a new world.

After years of separation from their homes and loved ones, many were able to readjust. Others could not pick up the pieces. Some who had been changed physically were met by partners willing to remember them as they had been and join them in their struggle. Others found themselves less welcome and the difficulties impossible to overcome. And still others found that the years apart had driven their mates into the comforting arms of new loves. Hundreds of thousands of children in Europe and even in Canada were left without a father, a mother or both.

And what of the work front?

Suddenly countless "Rosie the Riveters" who had laboured capably in wartime factories were pushed aside and forced to adopt "Doris Day roles" as homemakers. The returning heroes reclaimed the jobs they felt were rightfully theirs. Officers accustomed to salutes discovered that the pavements they had to pound in their job searches were much harder than parade squares.

Did you have any of these experiences? Were you a returning serviceman or woman who vividly recalls your homecoming? Or were you one of the unsung heroes who waited at home for the war to end?

Ben Wicks would love to hear from you to consider publishing your own account in his next book, *The Homecoming*.

Please write and tell us your story:
Ben Wicks
c/o Stoddart Publishing Co. Limited
34 Lesmill Road
Toronto, Canada
M3B 2T6